Grief
and Loss
in Schools

Grief and Loss in Schools

A RESOURCE FOR TEACHERS

Second Edition

Hazel Edwards

amba
press

First published in 1992
This second edition was published in 2023

Published by Amba Press
Melbourne, Australia
www.ambapress.com.au

Cover designer – Tess McCabe
Proofreader – Megan Bryant

ISBN: 9781922607447 (pbk)
ISBN: 9781922607454 (ebk)

A catalogue record for this book is available from the National Library of Australia.

CONTENTS

ABOUT THE AUTHOR

Hazel Edwards, OAM, is an award-winning author of books for children, teachers and adults.

An avid reader, as a young girl, Hazel Edwards wrote her first novel in grade six, a mystery about adventurous children stuck in a mine. This passion for writing continued after working in a secondary school and lecturing at teachers' college.

Aged twenty-seven, Hazel published her first novel, *General Store*, a book based on life in a rural town. It is Hazel's third published work that is her best known, the children's picture book classic, *There's a Hippopotamus on Our Roof Eating Cake*. This special imaginary friend has been cherished by children and parents alike and led to the dubious honour of Hazel being referred to as 'the Hippo Lady'.

Since its publication in 1980, the ageless *There's a Hippopotamus on Our Roof Eating Cake* has been reprinted annually, evolved into a series of seven picture books, inspired a junior chapter book, classroom play scripts, a musical stage production and a short movie. The Hippopotamus books have also been translated into Mandarin, Braille and Auslan signing for the hearing impaired and were presented as an official Australian Government gift to the children of Princess Mary of Denmark.

Whilst Hazel loves creating quirky, feisty characters for independent readers in her easy-to-read junior chapter books, she writes for all ages and has published over 220 books across a range of subjects and genres.

Published titles include *f2m:the boy within* the first co-written, young adult novel about gender transition, picture book *Stickybeak* and the co-written *Hijabi Girl* series now performed by Larrikin Puppets.

Hazel has collaborated with experts to publish adult non-fiction titles such as such as *Difficult Personalities* (translated into seven languages), and helps people craft interesting memoirs and family histories in her popular workshops based on her book *Writing a Non-Boring Family History*. More recently a 'Complete Your Book in a Year' course has been offered via Zoom.

Awarded the Australian Antarctic Division Arts Fellowship (2001), Hazel travelled to Casey Station on the 'Polar Bird' ice-ship. This visit inspired a range of creative projects including the young adult eco-thriller *Antarctica's Frozen Chosen*, picture book *Antarctic Dad* and the memoir, *Antarctic Writer on Ice*, as well as classroom playscripts.

A fan of interesting and unusual locations, Hazel has been a guest writer-in-residence in communities across Australia, a visiting author to Pasir Ridge International School in Indonesia and an author ambassador to Youfu West Street International School in China.

Passionate about literacy and creativity, Hazel has mentored gifted children and proudly held the title of Reading Ambassador for various organisations. Formerly a director on the Committee of Management of the Australian Society of Authors, Hazel was awarded an OAM for Literature in 2013. She is the patron of the Society of Women Writers (Vic) and in 2022 she was awarded the Monash University Distinguished Alumni Award for Education.

INTRODUCTION

We have to cope with change in our daily lives, but the shock associated with death and loss makes additional demands on our personal resources.

Are you, your class and school prepared to deal with the unexpected loss of a student, a teacher, or a parent associated with the school?

How can you provide support for your students after a death has occurred? It could be the death of a pet, a close friend, a relative or even a sporting hero.

In some classrooms, death, grief, and loss are taboo subjects. Many teachers and students feel uncomfortable about such topics and often avoid them until circumstances force attention.

This book aims to support teachers and schools when dealing with grief, loss, bereavement and a host of other feelings due to difficult change.

Chapter 1 provides discussion on a range of topics for educators and teachers to consider for their classroom. This chapter also includes a range of templates for correspondence to help you find the right words in a difficult time.

Chapter 2 is full of interesting and engaging activites for a range of age groups, year levels and circumstances. These activities can be easily added to lesson plans and will allow the students to work through some of the thoughts they are having.

The heart of this book, Chapter 3, provides a range of scripts for student engagement and discussion. The presence of a script is reassuring because there is something to 'talk around'. These scripts and stories can be used in a variety of ways and are full of discussion points and extension activities.

While everyone finds their own way to grieve through loss, it's important to have the support of friends and family, or someone else to talk to about the loss when needed. We hope you find a variety of ideas and activities to support your students and your school at this difficult time.

CHAPTER 1

RESOURCES

Timing

Sensitive topics require careful timing. Teachers are aware, on certain days, of the pointlessness of trying to discuss a topic such as handling grief or death. You have to choose your moment with the class.

But you may never know when a student from your class is likely to be touched by death, through personal accident or by relatives who die. The chances are that a teacher, a student or a pet associated with your school may die during the year.

Handling grief is related not only to death, it also covers the loss of friends through moving to another house, school or country, and coping with changes brought by separation, divorce or remarriage of parents. Grief can be associated with growing into a new age group and leaving behind 'younger' ways of doing things. You may have refugee or asylum seeker students who have traumatic pasts. Or those with domestic violence at home. And those whose parents are incarcerated in prison or camps.

How will you handle the situation in your classroom? If you are unsure, this is a good reason for working out some strategies for coping before a possible tragedy arises.

For members of the school community, the relevant question is:

What is bereavement and grief likely to mean in the classroom?

The Stages of Grief

Psychologists agree that we pass through certain kinds of feelings, or stages of grief as we come to terms with major change such as death. Different groups may give them different labels but these are the common stages:

- Acknowledging the pain of grief. This may include anger or even disbelief before the acknowledgement is made;
- Accepting the lost relationship as a reality. This may take weeks, months or even years;
- Adjusting to an environment minus that significant person. Again the time-span depends upon the individual;
- Redirecting time and energy from the lost relationship into something new. This may take several years.

Bereavement is the period of adjustment to loss. This period is elastic, depending upon the individual, but certain cultures allow a specified time for official acknowledgement of the bereavement.

Grief describes our feelings and reactions. These may fluctuate in intensity.

One student defined grief as "... things that go wrong in your life."

Classroom Decisions

If a student has died:

- Do you rearrange the desks so the vacant seat is not so obvious?
- Do you leave his/her work up on the display board?
- Do you distribute the class photo which includes the student who has died?
- What happens when the dead student's jumper is found when lost property is checked?

All of these examples have been mentioned by teachers as classroom decisions which have had to be made.

One teacher found it more acceptable to discuss with the class whether they wanted the desks changed or not. Their decision was 'yes', but not until the end of term.

The missing student's work was left on the display board for the normal length of time. 'Amy did that work when she was part of our class.'

The class photograph was seen by parents as being very precious, because it contained their missing student. Every student wanted to keep theirs.

When they were asked, the parents donated the 'lost' jumper to the pool of spare school clothing for use during wet weather. They wanted it to be of practical use to another student.

'I wish it hadn't happened in the holidays because holidays are for fun.' This was one student's immediate reaction to the death of a former classmate due to a road accident.

Reactions

It is possible to group children's likely reactions to grief according to their ages while making allowance for individual differences.

Up to about 2 years: the child is aware of separation and expresses feelings of loss, but detailed explanations are unnecessary.

Pre-schoolers: death is accepted as temporary and the child may not seem overly upset. A brief explanation may have be repeated, for example, life (eating, breathing, moving) has stopped, the deceased cannot feel anything, the body is buried and the deceased cannot come back to life.

Six to nine years: there is curiosity about cemeteries, funerals and other rituals. Details of death fascinate. They realise that death is final and all living things die.

Nine years plus: wider views on life and death begin to develop. Since adolescence is a period of uncertainty, teenagers need to face the loss openly (especially if another young person dies) in order that they can develop techniques of coping. Otherwise, fears and confusion will grow.

Individual reactions vary. Some will hit out, either verbally or physically. Others will go quiet. For a few, there will be a delayed reaction.

Some children or adolescent friends feel aggrieved because emphasis is placed only on the immediate family's emotional needs.

'We were her best friends; we need to be listened to as well.'

It is suggested that the class of the dead student be told before the rest of the school. Allow the students to attend the funeral if they wish. This is a goodbye ritual which makes it easier to accept the death later.

Plan together how to commemorate the student's life, for example, compile a book of memories and photos to give to the parents. Often there are hundreds of photographs of which the parents are un-aware. One class released balloons as a sign of freedom and farewell. Others have planted a memorial tree or garden in the school grounds.

Teacher Sensitivity

If you have not experienced personal grief before, you may be apprehensive about how to treat a recently bereaved student. It is common to feel helpless or uncertain about the best way to handle the situation. Act the way you genuinely feel. Try to listen. Remember that you can help create an accepting atmosphere in the classroom. Often other students are not sure how to react to the student who has lost a parent or a sibling. Your example will guide them.

First consider how the student is being treated at home.

- Is the student encouraged to take part in family farewells, such as viewing the deceased or attending the funeral? How does the student feel about this?
- Does the student know what is involved in a funeral service? Is the student aware that it is likely that people will be upset and crying at the funeral?
- Has a friend or relative been organised to stay with the student during the service and answer any questions?
- Is anyone listening to the student's fears: 'I'm scared to go to sleep in case I die like Gran'?
- Are family members sharing their grief by showing they are sad/ lonely/crying because someone important to them has died? This is likely to reassure the student that it is normal to feel and express sadness.
- How are outbursts of grief handled in the home?
- If the student screams, wets the bed, daydreams, or loses interest in food, how are these handled? Loving reassurance through cuddles and smiles is needed, not punishment.

Among primary-aged students, certain reactions are common after trauma. You may notice:

- Students role-playing the event with considerable detail;
- Short concentration span;
- Inconsistent behaviour,
- Fear of showing emotions, of being angry or crying;
- Specific fears triggered by reminders of the trauma, for example, fear of matches after a friend's recent third-degree burns.

How should you react? With understanding. It may take weeks or even months. Rather than being labelled as 'naughtiness', the students reactions are related to the past trauma. If the nature of the reactions become destructive, seek professional help.

Death of a Teaching Colleague

Grief can disable. It may take all a person's strength to keep up daily requirements such as getting dressed.

Often females find it easier to share their feelings and cry openly. Where there are 'macho' workplace expectations it will be harder for males to admit their hurt and ask for help.

> *"The Grade 4 teacher's wife drowned in a friend's swimming pool. He came back to work straight after the funeral. The next week he was a zombie. I found him staring at the roll while the kids were running riot. So we did some team teaching for a bit to lighten his load. I took his kids for swimming because he couldn't face the water. Later I listened while he started to unwind But it took most of the term before he was functioning at even fifty per cent."*

The greatest trap is to ignore a person's loss because of your own feelings of inadequacy. Common grief reactions include:

- Being accident prone
- Numbness and disbelief
- Crying
- Anger
- Depression
- Resentment (why me?)
- Loneliness
- Anxiety about the future.

Physically this may show in:

- 'Opting out' socially
- Tiredness
- Irritability
- Mood changes
- Frustration.

Death in a colleague's family may have a direct impact on your school. Child-care, transport and availability for after-school meetings and extra-curricular activities may change radically. The bereaved teacher may feel guilty, embarrassed, or oblivious to the changes. Suggestions about home help or family day-care may be relevant. Self-confidence is also affected by grief. Flexibility and patience can provide a supportive atmosphere.

Discourage quick major changes like selling houses or changing jobs. Changed behaviour such as drinking, smoking or drug-taking provide only temporary relief from responsibilities or painful memories.
Death is not the only loss. Grief may also be associated with:

- Unemployment
- Demotion
- Marital breakdown
- Bankruptcy
- Loss of a limb
- Terminal illness.

What Can I Do to Help?

A caring environment in a school can help support the griever.

- Keep in touch.
- Say little on a first visit. Touch may be enough.
- Avoid repeating clichés such as 'He's better off now'.
- Be natural, even if you cry too.
- Accept silence or be a good listener.
- Don't presume to tell the bereaved how s/he feels.
- Don't probe for details about the death.
- Avoid talking to others about trivial subjects, for example shopping prices, in front of the recently bereaved.
- Don't comment on 'unusual behaviour' such as repeated visits to the grave site.
- Write a personal letter rather than send a commercial sympathy card.
- Often the best way to help is just to listen!

School-wide Trauma

In one school there were three deaths during one term: a student from a traffic accident nearby; a teacher's from a heart attack; a parent closely associated with the school, who died from cancer.

Action will vary according to the age of those involved, whether the incident was public, and the extent of involvement.

Anything beyond our normal ability to cope with can be traumatic, including bushfire, flood, or mass evacuation.

Suggested approach

1. As co-ordinator of recovery, the school principal's role is to liaise with emergency services and the families of those affected.
2. Provide information to those affected by the trauma. Understanding the facts rather than worrying about rumours gives a sense of control.
3. Resume normal duties as soon as possible, once the event has been officially acknowledged through a memorial service or an announcement.
4. Assess the psychological needs of those affected.

If a tragedy has occurred, it's best to let other parents know the facts immediately. A letter to parents needs to tell:

- The facts
- What the school has done
- What help is available
- How their students may react.

The First Class Afterwards

It is best to sit in a circle to allow everyone to share others' reactions.

- Allow the students to tell you what happened.
- Distinguish between facts and rumours.
- If moved to tears, share them rather than hide them.

- Discuss: 'How did you feel? Where were you when it happened?'
- How might others feel now?
- Allow the students time to express and 'normalise' their reactions.
- Have clay and drawing materials available if some need to express feelings in a different medium.
- Plan how survivors returning to school will be supported or how cards and messages can be sent during their absence.
- Tell the students what help is available. End positively, for example, 'What can we do immediately for the victims and families?'
- Plan a follow-up time.

Individual Counselling and Small Groups

There is a difference between counselling one student and caring for a large group who are mourning.

Peer support is important. Small grief groups of 3-4 provide a sense of safety, as many will not reveal their genuine feelings in a larger group. Even an agreement of confidentiality will help some children to talk honestly about their feelings.

How to Write a Eulogy

Basically a 'eulogy' means saying nice things about the person who has died, and to celebrate their life. 'Eu' means good 'in ancient Greek language'.

Speaking in public is the greatest fear for many people. But this is where notes from existing family history research are often useful.

The hardest eulogy to give is for a young person and especially one who has died unexpectedly.

The family may be relieved if you offer to speak on behalf of the school community, even if you are not of their religion or culture.

Maybe you will speak at the school assembly.

Alternatively, the eulogy may be digital and visual. Photos from the person's life, even without captions, flicking through with appropriate music.

There are two parts to a eulogy; writing and then delivering it, usually at the funeral.

To write a eulogy, you need to gather the facts of the person's life quickly: dates of birth, years when people worked where, and the correct names of colleagues. Others may help, but the eulogy writer has to craft it. And it's a more personal tribute, if you 'profile' the life of the person you knew well, rather than a stranger just reading it, even if you do get upset. Often a funeral celebrant will advise on compiling the short talk or will even talk at the ceremony around the notes you have provided. However, these hints may help in the writing.

- Check if any family members are compiling a history. Copy the facts.
- Display dated and captioned family photos at the ceremony. Put on a digital show, as it gives people something to talk about.
- Anecdotes are mini stories, often humorous. Jot down 5–6 anecdotes or memories which typify that person for you because they symbolise attributes e.g. good organiser/sense of humour/ persistent. Tell the best first, to set the tone.

- Keep the sentences short and number the points.
- Print it off in really large, dark font so you can read through tears or glasses.
- Focus on the person, not only your relationship to them.
- Find a theme or linking idea e.g. A practical person who finished projects.
- Consider your audience, some may not know all aspects of that life, so you need to tell stories in context. For example, explain who Aunty Mary was.
- The age of the person who died determines the type of audience. If they have out-lived their contemporaries, had little family and not belonged to organisations, the numbers may be small. But if well known and died young, there may be many contributing eulogies for various aspects of a life: family, work, sport, membership of organisations, community work.
- Often some facts of a life are news at a funeral for some audience members. Be diplomatic.
- Allude to weaknesses, but with acceptance e.g. had a short fuse.
- A spoken funeral eulogy is often used as the basis of a published obituary later.
- Sometimes there's a mismatch and the eulogist does not really make appropriate tribute to the person's life. Or the eulogist may be brilliant in the writing and delivery and make a hero out of someone who wasn't.
- The tone needs to be genuine. Even if you break down, the audience will feel with you.
- Practise reading and keep to a time limit. Brief is better.
- Send a copy to the family afterwards, for their family history. Write with your heart, but you also need to craft it.

Sample Correspondence

Principal to Parents – Death of a Student

Dear Parents and Carers,

Yesterday, one of our students was killed in a tragic road accident while returning from the Year 6 school camp.

… was with 27 other Year 6 students in a bus when it slipped on the icy Mountain View Road near …, went out of control and rolled down the hill.

One teacher, Miss …, has been badly hurt and is in intensive care at … Hospital. Some students were slightly injured but all were allowed home after medical treatment.

I have visited the parents of … and extended to them the condolences of our whole school community. In addition I have offered any support we are able to give.

We intend to hold a memorial service for … at school on Monday afternoon at 2.30 pm in the Assembly Hall. Further details will be sent soon.

Although your sons and daughters will be affected by the death of our student, it would be best for them to resume school routines as soon as possible.

Students' reactions will vary and may include crying, not wanting to talk (or excessive talking), anger, lack of concentration, sleeping or eating problems. Should you feel that your child needs professional counselling, contact me at the school.

Yours sincerely,

Principal

Dear Parents and Carers,

As principal, I have some very sad news.

Our school community suffered a great loss yesterday afternoon when one of our Prep students Pip Nguyen died in a tragic car accident outside the school gates at 3.30 pm.

Pip was hit by a car and died in the ambulance on the way to hospital. Her parents were with her.

Our condolences go to Pip's family and the school has immediately offered to help them in every way possible. Counsellors and interpreters are available.

It's possible that your child saw the accident and is very upset.

Our counsellors and staff are available for your child, your family and the community.

How can you help your child? Listen to them. Allow them to ask questions, even if you find it difficult to answer. It's all right to say you don't know. And that you feel so sad too. It's okay to cry and be upset. Pip's teacher will be available before and after school this week and an announcement will be made to students at school assembly tomorrow.

Pip's family will be supported by all of us. As principal, I am available too. And we will share with you any plans for a memorial to Pip in which students may be involved.

But it's important for you to be aware of the facts and also the ways in which there is help available today for our students and families. Our community has lost Pip, and we are all grieving. Our thoughts are with Pip's parents, family and her classmates especially.

Yours sincerely,

Principal

Class Teacher to Parents – Death of a Student

Dear Parents and Carers,

I'm ..., the Prep teacher and Pip was one of my students.

We all miss her smiling face and laugh. She loved Art best at school.

We would like to involve students in designing a sympathy card in Art class tomorrow.

This is a way of helping them express their feelings and may comfort Pip's parents.

It's possible that your family may have group photos on your mobile/camera which include Pip but which her parents have not seen.

Would you allow us to use copies of these in a memory album to give Pip's family? The class will also have a copy of the album in our classroom library shelf.

Later we would like to make a garden in her memory, using plants with a special meaning for Pip and her family.

You are welcome to be involved and it may help express the grief we all share.

Yours,

Teacher

Principal to Parents – Death of a Staff Member

Dear Parents and Carers,

As principal, I have some very sad news.

Our school community suffered a great loss yesterday afternoon when your child's teacher ... was involved in a tragic accident during an excursion to ... While saving a student, the teacher lost his own life.

.... has been a highly respected educator and his colleagues have always admired how he cared for his students. Their welfare came first and he was very safety conscious. His death is a great loss to his family and to the school community.

We are all shocked and our condolences have gone to his family and we are trying to help in every way.

It's important for you to know the facts of what happened, as the incident is likely to be on the TV news. The student is bruised but not seriously injured and was taken to hospital. The excursion staff team were supportive. Students are being counselled and the excursion finished early. Temporarily, Ms Brown who is also a counsellor will take over ... role at the school. She will be available to speak with parents anytime.

... family will make private arrangements for 'a celebration of life' ceremony for ... and the school community may be involved.

You can best help your child, by allowing opportunities to talk about their teacher, make a memorial card or just give permission to be sad. Accept any crying or even atypical behaviour. All of us grieve in different ways. It may be small changes in the classroom which make a student upset, after the loss of their teacher. But Ms Brown and the rest of our staff will share in supporting your child.

This is a shock to all of us.

Principal

Principal/Teacher to Parent – Death of their Child

Dear Mr and Mrs ...,

We are sorry to hear of the death of ... He was a very special student and his class and I will miss him.

We will always remember him as a fun-loving student with a great sense of humour. My favourite memory is seeing his face light up at the sight of the zebras when we went to the zoo. I'll never forget his smile.

It must be very difficult for you at present. Let me know if you'd like some help in any way. He will be missed by the school and his class. He'll always live in our memories.

Thinking of you and your family,

Teacher/Principal

Chapter 2

Activities

Educators are always time-poor and need quick ideas which can be adapted in emergency situations.

Maybe a tragedy occurred in the school community and you need to share ways to help your students? Or your community may have suffered mass evacuations and disruptions due to flood, fire or accidents, and the disorientated students need ways to process their losses? Refugee students from war zones may have joined your school? Or your school may be preparing in case a tragic situation arises?

A range of activities which can be slotted into a day's lesson plans, will enable more students to find ways of handling their personal loss in a wider perspective. Whereas writing and performing scripts enable indirect discussion of the sensitive issues as a group, long term.

Some won't want to write but can draw. Some need to talk but not about themselves. So an indirect discussion may help.

Changes

Big changes happen in everyone's lives. Some changes make you happy. Some changes make you sad.

What are some of the changes happening in your life which make you feel happy?

1.
2.
3.

What are some of the changes which make you feel sad?

1.
2.
3.

Wishes

Have you ever wished that you could change things in your life?

If you were given three wishes, what would they be?

What are some of the changes that could matter for you?

Sad, Sad, Sad

What makes you feel sad?

What is the saddest thing that has happened to you?

What did you do afterwards?

If someone else was sad, would you:

- Talk to them?
- Listen to them?
- Give them a hug?
- Ask them to play?
- Do something else?

Happy, Happy, Happy

What makes you feel happy?

What is the happiest thing that has happened to you?

What did you do afterwards?

1.
2.
3.

Lost

Have you ever lost:

- Someone close to you?
- Favourite belongings?
- Your self-confidence?
- Part of your body, e.g. finger, hair or leg?
- Some of your past (e.g. when leaving your home town or changing households)?
- The country where you were born?

Consider:

- How did you feel?
- What did you do?
- Did anyone help you? What did they do?
- Was anything that someone said especially helpful at that time?
- What was said?

What are some of the things which made or make you feel better:

1.
2.
3.

Goldie

Your goldfish has died. Goldie was your favourite pet. You found Goldie floating on the top of the water.

Do you feel:

- Sad?
- Angry?
- Like crying?
- Guilty that you didn't check earlier?
- You don't want to think about it?

Draw a book of things you remember about your fish.

Flowers

Draw your favourite flower. Explain why it is your favourite.

Certain flowers have special meanings, such as red roses for love.

Often flowers are given:

- To celebrate
- To make you feel better
- To show the giver cares.

Flowers are often given or carried at:

- Birthdays
- Parties
- Hospitals
- Weddings
- Funerals.

Which flower would you be given most, and why?

Moving

"We're moving at the end of the month."

What will have to be done?

- Pack up clothes and toys.
- Say goodbye to friends.
- Leave your old school.
- Start a new school.

Make a list of things to be done. How do you feel about doing these?

Things to be done	How I feel	Why I feel like this
•	•	•
•	•	•
•	•	•

Goodbye Book

Alex is leaving your school.

Make a book for Alex to take. You might include illustrations or photographs of:

- Alex's friends
- Alex's favourite place to play (under the basketball ring)
- The classroom
- His teacher
- The class photograph
- Things Alex likes doing (playing basketball, making things in art, playing the drums, mucking around)
- Things Alex doesn't like doing (picking up papers, spelling tests)
- Fun things that happened while Alex was here
- Alex's most embarrassing moment (his pants split).

Give the book to Alex; or if he has already left, send it to his parents.

Making a BUT Book

This is a fill-the-gap book.

Write how you feel in the space.

I feel sad when ...

BUT I feel better when .....

I feel it is my fault when ...

BUT I know it isn't because ...

Time Out

What do you most like doing?

If you had only 24 more hours, would you:

- Spend it with friends?
- Say sorry to some people?
- Stay with your family?
- Do something dangerous?
- Go to sleep?
- Do something you've always wanted to do?

Draw five things that you most like doing.

Try Huggling

What ...

- Doesn't cost money?
- Has power without batteries?
- Isn't fattening?
- Can't be taxed?
- Doesn't pollute?
- Can be recycled?
- And is fully returnable?

Answer: A huggle

What is a huggle?

- A huggle is something between a hug and a cuddle
- Can you hug?
- Can you cuddle?
- A huggle is both at once.

You Can't Say 'Dead' Nicely

A 'euphemism' is a way of avoiding words which make us feel uncomfortable. Because many adults find it hard to say 'dead' or 'death', other words are used to describe the fact that someone has died.

Have you heard comments like:

- "Grandma has gone."
- "Uncle is far away."
- "Your baby brother is a star in the sky. You can see them twinkle." ("But what about on cloudy nights? Where is he?")
- "He's helping God in his garden."
- "She's sleeping forever." ("Will that happen to me when I go to bed to sleep tonight?')
- "He's lost his grandmother." ("Was he careless?")
- "He passed away."

What is said in your family, if someone dies?

How do you feel about using the word 'dead'?

'Dead' is a Four-Letter Word

We use 'dead' in ordinary conversation, but we don't always mean someone has died (e.g. Does that street have a dead end?).

- Are you dead sure? Are you dead certain about that?
- The ball was dead centre!
- Drive dead ahead. You can't miss it.
- Our house is burglar-proof; the door has a dead lock?

Are there any other dead words or phrases you know? Make a list.

Why do you think that each came to be used? Was it something to do with stopping?

Song-writer

You are a song-writer.

Your latest song has gone to the top of the charts. Now you've been asked to write a new song. This will be called 'Missing.'

'Missing' is about feeling sad because someone will never come back. Write the words (lyrics) for the first verse.

What type of musical backing might you need? Or will you use other sound effects?

How do you want the audience to feel after hearing your song?

- Glad that someone else feels that way?
- Sad?
- Happy?

The mood of the music needs to fit the subject of the song. How is a feeling of sadness shown? By fast music? Slow music? Long notes? Repetition? Is a chorus used?

Imagine if you want to share a sad feeling. Which musical instruments might fit the mood?

- Piano?
- Trumpet?
- Violin?
- Guitar?

If you wanted to share a happier mood, how could you do this? Which musical instruments might you use? What songs might you play?

Leaving Home

Migrants, asylum seekers and refugees who leave their countries often feel sad. They are not just leaving a place, they are also leaving friends and familiar ways of doing things.

There are many songs and folksongs about 'leaving'.

Find an example. Discuss their experience and how it made them feel.

Q&A Turned Around

Often you are asked a question and expected to give an answer. This is the other way around. If each of these is an answer, what might the question have been?

- Confused about what happened
- Scared it might happen to you
- Sad
- Missing
- Crying
- Lonely
- Sick
- Happy
- Making a friend

Memorial Garden

Why do some people plant a tree or design a garden in memory of a person?

- Design a memorial garden.
- Name the garden.
- Will you have a seat?
- Water feature?
- What type of plants or trees? Colours? Shapes?

Memories

What things do you want to do or be in your life that others will remember you by?

- Create a game
- Being a good friend
- Teach a younger kid how to do something
- Build a bridge
- Design a building
- Invent something
- Solve a problem that helps your community
- Cure diseases
- Work out a better system for doing an ordinary job
- Operate on others eyes so that they can see
- Show people how to get along better
- Something else

Why do you want them to remember this?

Why is it important?

Compliments /Memories Jar

Find an attractive container. Each student writes one nice thing about the person, reads it aloud, folds and adds it to the decorated jar.

Give the jar to the family.

Legacy

A legacy is something you leave behind when you die.

What would you like to leave behind that would be useful for others?

What are the 3 words you'd like people to use about you:

- Generous
- Fun
- Sporty
- Kind
- Problem-solver
- A good trier?

What are 3 words to describe the person who died?

- Good listener
- Best friend
- Likeable or loveable because ...
- Always helpful
- Willing to try
- Aometimes grumpy/quiet/tired because of the illness

To extend this activity you could discuss remembering a person's legacy on their anniversary. An anniversary is on the same date often a year later. It may be the date the person died. Their birthday. Or the date of a ritual which was important to their family.

In what ways could you remember the person on that special date? It may be enough for you to mention that you remember their significant date.

Quiet Heros

The actions of quiet heroes are often known only by those they have helped. Maybe only you know how kind your brother was to other kids. Or your friend? Or your relative?

Today the term 'hero' is used for any gender. A hero solves a problem for a community, acts as a good role model, is a leader with ideas or works out better ways of doing things.

Who is your hero?

What do you remember them for?

Is being a 'celeb' the same as being a hero?

No. A 'celeb' or 'celebrity' is famous only for getting their photo into the media or being 'fashionable'.

Being a celebrity is not the same as being known for your heroic achievements or solving problems for others.

A genuine 'hero' may be in the news, but it's for what they have done, not what they are wearing or for misbehaving.

Some heroes act bravely in an emergency. This is fast courage.

Others persist and do things a little better each day. Long term, their actions may influence many people.

Some heroes are role models, without even realising. They are not perfect, but they can inspire others to copy what they do, or to do their own best, even under difficult circumstances. Like all of us, they have strengths and weaknesses but heroes try hard and are passionate about what they do.

Hypothetical

Hypothetical is a big word for an ideas game.

Ask 'What if?' and play with ideas as a way of solving a problem. Often it's done in a group, with someone pulling the ideas together. Players can all have different views.

Accept all suggestions. Others can build on those ideas.

Some hypothetical situations to discuss:

- If a student has died, should the classroom be rearranged so their empty place is not so obvious? Or should you leave it empty in their memory? What about their name peg where their backpack used to hang? Or their appearance in class photos?
- Should you go to a memorial service of another culture, if you're unsure of the correct practices to follow?
- Should you light a candle or perform a ritual in a religious place where you don't belong, but where a memorial is being held?
- Which words are acceptable for use to explain that a person has died?

Make a Word Sandwich

Write or draw something to go in the middle of the word sandwich.

Opening sentence:

It was a day I would never forget.

Last sentence:

That was the good thing which happened, even on a sad day.

Expressions of Sympathy

When someone dies, friends often send cards or letters to the family saying how much the person will be missed. These are called sympathy cards or letters of condolence.

Some commercial sympathy cards verses are not as personal as if you were to write your own. Use a plain card or one with an appropriate picture.

Dear Chris,

I was sorry to hear of the death of your father. He was a very special person and we'll all miss him.

I'll always remember him as a kind man with a great sense of humour. My favourite memory is when we went on that boating trip together. I'll never forget how kind he was after I fell in the water.

It must be very difficult for you at present. Let me know if you'd like some help in any way. I'm sure he must have been a very special man to have produced such a family He'll always live in our memories.

Thinking of you and your family,
Billie Roy

A letter of condolence tries to comfort the person who has lost someone or something. Generally it is handwritten rather than typed, as this is considered more personal.

What would you like friends to write about you?

- A good friend who will be missed
- Someone who cared
- A good worker
- A good parent or sister/brother
- Remembered for your smile
- A good team member
- Something else?

Obituaries, Funeral and Death Notices

Obituaries, funeral and death notices are listed in the newspaper and online. Names are listed in alphabetical order of the surname.

Families announce news of important changes in a person's life into the paper or online so that others will know.

When you were born, your parents probably put a notice in the newspaper or on social media. The birth notice named your parents, said where you were born, how much you weighed, your new name (if chosen yet) and how they felt about your birth. Sometimes grandparents or other relatives put in a notice to say how they feel about your birth.

When a person dies, a death notice is placed in the newspaper or on social media. It says where the person died, and whether by accident or through illness. Friends and relatives often express how they feel about the person.

Next day, there is usually a funeral notice to give details of where and when the funeral will be held, so friends can attend or send flowers.

Look at a newspaper online. Check the notices.

- Have any significant people died recently and an obituary written about them?
- Is there an alphabetical list of the names of people who have died in the past few days? What kind of information is given in these notices?

Case Studies

These people have written their stories for you and your students to share. They tell how they feel.

Discuss each case with your group. Their individual responses can be oral or written. Some may prefer to draw their answers or even role play.

My Hair Fell Out!

My name is Ifram and I am twelve. I have been diagnosed with leukaemia for the past one and a half years, I have been good with my treatment, tablets and injections for a whole year.

At the start I was coughing a lot and had a sore throat. Then I started to feel horrible. At nights I couldn't sleep and I had stomach pains.

Mum took me to the doctor and at first they thought it was just the flu which was going around. Later, the doctors became suspicious and kept me in hospital under observation and did some tests.

I didn't even know what the word leukaemia meant then. The treatment made me put on weight and my hair fell out. The kids at school gave me a hard time about being bald, so I started wearing a cricket cap all the time. For this Christmas I would like to have the Cricket Test Match game but I can't buy it because it costs $85.

Yet the only thing I really want is to get better. I have been to the Royal Children's Hospital for treatment lots of times. The doctors say I might be cured. I have to go back in January for some new tests.

What can I do to stop the other kids teasing me about my hair, or lack of it?

If Ifram was in your class, would you:

- Play with him?
- Talk to him about the illness?
- Listen when he talks about his hospital visits?
- Just treat him like any other kid?

How would you feel if all your hair fell out? Would you wear a cap, a wig or a scarf?

My Gran Taylor died last year.

I miss her. She used to tell me stories. And she let me stay up late. I used to go to her place after school. We had biscuits and apples for snacks. And we played games.

Now I have to go to Mrs Amit's place. We have yucky snacks there. And we watch television all the time.

I miss Gran Taylor. "Where is she now?" I asked Mum.

Mum looked upset. "She's up in the sky."

I wish Gran Taylor was back at Flat 1, Number 25 Station Street.

At Christmas time we flew to Queensland for a holiday. I'd never been on a plane before. There was something special I wanted to do. The flight attendant gave me the window seat. I put on my seat belt. The plane went up. I looked out of the window. I could see the sky.

It was blue with white clouds. But I couldn't see Gran Taylor.

I wonder where she is?

Discuss:

- Where did Gran Taylor used to live?
- Why did they like going there?
- Why were they looking out of the plane window?
- What would you say if a younger student asked you where a person had gone after they died?
- Why would you say that?

Saying 'Dead' Nicely Doesn't Help!

Miss Timms is our Grade 3/4 teacher. Last month she kept mice in the classroom. All the students helped to look after them. Mousey was in his cage next to my desk, I used to watch him.

Over the holidays, the mice multiplied. They even got into the staff room and ate the biscuits.

The mice all had names. On Monday, Mousey was found dead in his cage. He looked yukky and stiff. His whiskers stuck out. Maria the pet monitor cried.

We were pretty upset. None of our pets had died before.

We had a funeral for Mousey. Miss Timms found a box for a coffin. We lined the box with green tissue paper. We wrote a 'Goodbye Mousey' poem on the whiteboard.

We picked flowers to put on the coffin. Then we walked behind Miss Timms to the garden.

There was a hole in the flower bed. We put Mousey's coffin into the hole and covered it up. We took turns with the spade. Even Maria. I hated the noise of the spade.

Miss Timms says that Mousey will become part of the earth.

"Will he be a skeleton?"

Miss Timms said, "Yes. In a while."

"What happens after that?" Miss Timms didn't know.

We put a sign with 'Mousey' on the grave. We said things about Mousey. I talked about how I liked him living beside my desk. Maria said she liked the way his nose moved when she fed him.

Then we went inside. I felt better that we had said 'Goodbye.' But I still miss Mousey. Some students say he's gone or he's lost. Saying 'dead' nicely doesn't help.

Every time we play computers, and the mouse is used, I think of Mousey. What can I do about the way I feel?

Discuss:

- How would you answer the question in the last sentence?
- Why do some people use the other words instead of 'dead'?
- How do you think the funeral helped the students to cope with Mousey's death?

Dad, Where's Mum?

My name is Melinda. I am 12 years old. Last month, my Mum died. She had been sick for a long time.

I really miss her. Especially at 'getting-up' time, I wait to hear her shower. Then I remember. She's not here any more. Sometimes I cry in bed or in the shower, so Dad doesn't hear me.

I miss talking about her. Nobody wants to talk to me about her. They don't want me to talk about her either. It's as if they want her to vanish.

Kids at school freak out if mothers are mentioned. They look sideways at me to see how I'm taking it. If a word like 'death' or 'funeral' comes up in class, they all pretend not to look at me. I think they want to help me, but they don't know what to say, so they're treating me as if I'm stupid, or I don't hurt inside.

If I cry, they say, "Don't cry. Things will get better. Your Dad might get married again and you'll have another mother." Then I get angry. I don't want another Mum. I want mine back.

She can't just have stopped. She must be somewhere.

Dad, where's Mum?

Discuss:

- Melinda cries in the shower. Where would you cry if you didn't want others to hear?
- Is there anything that might worry you about others seeing or hearing you cry? Why do you think you feel this way about it?

- What might you say to someone whose mother has died?
- How might Melinda's Dad be feeling?
- How might Melinda help her Dad?
- How might Dad help Melinda?

Separation

They told me last night. My Mum and Dad aren't going to live together any more. Dad's leaving to live in a flat.

"What about me?" I asked. "Where am I going to live?" I felt all squeezed inside.

They are my Mum and Dad. They've been around all my life. They are my parents. How can they stop being that?

"We still love you. But we don't love each other any more." If they stopped loving each other, when are they going to stop loving me?

In bed last night I cried. Then I thought about what I could do. Maybe if I got up on time and made the breakfast, they'd stay. Mum was always yelling at me to do my jobs. Dad was always yelling at me about being late. Perhaps they were just tired of yelling?

I made the breakfast. But it didn't make any difference. Mum and Dad argued all the time. And our baby Janey screamed.

Inside, I screamed too.

There's a footy match at school next week. Students are playing teachers and parents. My Dad won't be there.

Discuss:

- Sometimes parents decide to part, but they still love their children. They may get divorced, but they don't divorce their children.
- What do you most like doing with your Mum or Dad?
- Do you like someone from home to watch you play sport or take part in things at school?

One of My Legs Didn't Feel Right

Over the holidays, I was in a car accident. Our car smashed into another car. My Mum was driving. I was sitting in the back seat. My seat belt was on.

"Look out!" yelled Mum. Then there was a bang.

Our car turned over. I was caught inside. I don't know what else happened. When I woke up in the hospital, one of my legs didn't feel right. Afterwards the doctor told me. My right leg was all twisted under the car. To save me, they had to take part of my right leg off. It's not fair!

That's my goal-kicking foot. The doctor said I can get an artificial leg soon. But I don't want to get a fake foot.

At first, when I went back to school, the other kids were okay. But now they forget when I can't keep up. And the crutches hurt my arms. Sports Day was the worst. Miss Smith made me Chief Scorer. It was the pits. All the other kids were in at least two races. I just sat there. They wouldn't even let me in the three-legged race!

I hate being called 'Hoppy' or 'Crutchy.' I wish I could make time go backwards like the button on the video.

Or even 'Fast Forward'!

Discuss:

- Have you ever been in an accident? How did you feel?
- If you had one leg, what might be hard for you to do?

Further Activities:

- Tie your arm in a sling. Wear the sling for one day. What is the hardest thing to do?
- Form pairs. Put a blindfold on one person. In pairs walk around the yard. The 'seeing' partner can tell the other where to go. What was the hardest thing to do?

Pets as Part of the Family

We've had Johnno for a long time, since he was a puppy.

He's part of our family.

But last Thursday, he ran out on to the road. A truck hit him. I heard the squeal of the brakes. Then I heard a thud. I raced over from the bus stop, but it was too late.

There was blood on the road. His body was all floppy.

The driver kept saying, "I'm sorry. I'm sorry."

But it wasn't really his fault. He helped me carry Johnno home.

I feel as if it was my fault. Johnno was waiting for me to get home from school. We always go for a walk together. But Thursday, I was mucking around with some kids at the bus shelter. So Johnno crossed to road to find me.

The vet said Johnno hadn't felt much. The truck was SO quick.

We buried him in our garden. Mum gave me a rose bush to plant on top. She loves roses. And she loved Johnno.

I wish I'd come straight home Thursday night. But Mum said Johnno's death wasn't my fault.

Discuss:

- What are some of the ways in which a pet can be remembered? What would you do?
- Can you understand why the student might feel blame for Johnno's death?

The Funeral Parlour: A Year Six Excursion

It may seem strange to have a regular 'funeral parlour' excursion for primary aged students, but I was invited to accompany one group as the funeral director had been a teacher previously, and we had worked together. The visit is explained here because the responses were so positive from educators, who found the students' genuine questions and the grief counsellor's tactful answers helpful.

"Hearses can have car crashes."

"There's a room where you can be alone with the dead person and put some of their special things into the coffin."

"Dead people can still grow a beard and toenails."

Intriguing evaluations of the funeral parlour visit came from students' written responses to the question.

"What were the ten most interesting things you found out today?"

Some spelling was idiosyncratic, 'berrying' (burying) or being 'castrated' (cremated) were the options as one student saw it.

Was the funeral parlour visit educationally worthwhile for the students?

"Very much so," said Rev. Laurie Barton, junior school chaplain of Carey Grammar. "They have their factual questions answered but also it makes them think about others' feelings."

Rev. Barton is one of a number of teachers who each year arranged for their Year Six students to visit the funeral parlour. This is part of the grief and loss subject within their school.

The students and accompanying teachers were taken, in two groups of fifteen, on a tour of the funeral parlour by a grief counsellor and the funeral parlour's marketing manager, a former teacher who reassured the students that they would not see any dead people on the premises that day. Death was a foreign concept to most of the 11- and 12-year-olds apart from one boy who mentioned his grandfather's funeral two years ago. At first, students were quietly apprehensive in the foyer.

"You do not have to go into any area that you do not wish to visit," reassured the counsellor. "At any time, you can just wait outside. It's no problem."

Display racks for flowers in the foyer were the first exhibit.

"Why do you think we have fold down racks instead of open shelves?"

The students thought for a while, reassured by this apparently normal and non-threatening thought.

"So the people who don't have many friends to send flowers don't feel bad."

"That's right." Then they moved into the chapel.

"In here, the family come to listen. Do you know what a speech about the person is called?"

"Eulogy" was a new word to all the students. They agreed it was nice for a special speaker to say good things about the person's life.

Then the 'viewing' was explained. 'We have the body here in a small room so that family and friends can say goodbye if they wish.

"Why is it only a small room?" asked a student.

An experienced ex-teacher, Russ, turned the question back on the student. "What do you think?"

"Not everybody might want to see," suggested the student.

"That's right."

The direct answers from the staff encouraged students to participate eagerly and honestly.

"What would happen if a shark ate everything except the finger of the person? Would you have a coffin for the little finger?"

Enthralled, the others leaned forward.

"Yes, if the family wished to do so. Often if there has been a tragic death and the body is missing, a family will hold a memorial service later, without a coffin. They may have only the ashes present."

"Do you have doctors?"

"No. A doctor's function is to preserve life. But a doctor at the hospital or elsewhere must sign a death certificate for the official records."

"Do you get upset at funerals?"

'Yes. If you get to the stage where you don't relate and get upset, you're in the wrong job."

The next question was very hesitant. "If a whole family all die in the one road accident, do you have just one coffin for them?"

"No. Legally there must be only one person per coffin, unless it is a mother and a very little baby. But we have room in our hearse to have two coffins side by side."

Differences between caskets and coffins were established. Coffins which are shaped to the body are used mainly in New Zealand and Australia. Caskets which are rectangular are more popular in America.

Two small girls were holding hands before going into the room where coffins and caskets were displayed. Diplomatically it was suggested that the students work out which was the dearest coffin. Distracted into comparing price tags, they calmed down, even feeling the fancy drapery of the lining. Then the metal coffin, with a fifty year water-tight guarantee arose interest.

"Any small coffins for babies who die?"

She nodded. "Children's coffins are usually white."

"Do you get emotional about baby coffins?"

"It would be very hard not to."

The counsellor showed the album with pictures of different types of coffins. "Sometimes the family comes in here to choose. Other times we go to the home, and we take the album to them."

One boy was still worried about money. "What if someone can't pay for their own funeral?"

"Friends or family usually help. Often the hat will go around at the club or community centre, or a crowdfunding website is set up. If there's still not enough, the government will give a state funeral. That's a very basic coffin and an unmarked grave. By law, bodies have to be buried or cremated."

A white hearse had been parked at the front door so the students could examine it. They were impressed by its $100,000 cost.

"How much do you have to pay to get a ride to the cemetery in the mourning car?" asked the boy who was still concerned about money.

Possibly because they only heard the word 'hearse' and didn't see it spelled, some got mixed up between 'his' and 'hers'. Another proclaimed "Hearses are just done up cars".

The cool room was most worrying to the students because of the medicinal smell and the actual freezer (empty). Again the counsellor distracted them by asking why the coffins were stored with the lids upside down. (To protect them from scratching.)

The respect with which the 'bodies' are handled and spoken of as 'the deceased' reassured the students and the teachers. Gory myths of recycled coffins and wreaths were dispelled.

Overall it was an eye-opening experience for everyone involved.

Chapter 3

Scripts

Scripting

In recent years I have been using scripts in schools as a way of stimulating student discussion. It seemed feasible to structure discussions of grief and loss in the same way. The presence of a script is reassuring because there is something to 'talk around'.

These scripts:

- Allow the reader to identify with a problem through the character's reactions;
- Help students to realise they are not alone;
- Lead to the sharing of problems;
- Provide opportunities for small groups to discuss personal worries during rehearsals;
- Offer the opportunity to identify with others' situations;
- Initiate the topic of loss with parents at home, whilst they are preparing costumes or scripts for the performance;

- Provide a cathartic experience, by allowing the discharge of repressed emotions;
- Help students to cope with loss.

The Material

It was technically challenging to write this material. As well as doing considerable background reading, I interviewed school chaplains and listened to the experiences of people who had coped with loss. Then I had to shape the material to make it readily accessible. My personal guidelines were:

- Is the script an honest and accurate portrayal of experiences of grief?
- Is the script likely to open discussion on a sensitive topic?
- Will the content transcend any modes of religious or cultural thinking?
- Will it work as a play? Can the script be performed in an average classroom? Are there sufficient roles? Is there an underlying conflict (apart from life versus death) which is being resolved? Does enough happen? Is the language suitable for the age group?

How to Create a Script

Writing scripts is a good way of working out your ideas on a topic.

Form groups of 4-5 people.

Discussion

- **Ideas** – What do you want to share with the audience? Example, how people feel about losing a class pet.
- **Theme** – What is the major idea you are exploring? Is there an underlying conflict?
- **Title** – Does it tell what the play is about? Does the title attract attention?

- **Cast** – How many? Will you need a narrator or a chorus? Make the cast names sound different, for example, don't have a Jane and a Janie.
- **Props** – As few as possible.
- **SFX (special effects)** – Will any sound effects be needed?
- **Setting** – Where will the play happen? At what time?
- **Script** – Does the opening introduce the characters quickly? Do they have enough to do? The plot is the 'what happens next'? What is your plot?
- **Ending** – How will your play end? Is there a 'twist'?

Now write your play script. One person can be the scribe and take notes. Don't forget that you may need to make changes after workshopping your script.

Using Scripts in the Classroom

When 'The Memory Bank Robbers' was created at Jordanville South Primary there were three main stages:

- Idea mongering
- Rough draft
- Workshopping.

See pages 72–81 for the full script of 'The Memory Bank Robbers'.

Idea Mongering

First, questions were asked to provoke brainstorming around the words *Memory Bank*.

What does a memory bank make you think about?

Responses included:

- Brain box
- Computer memory bank
- A bank where you deposit your feelings
- A bank run by Mr Memory.

What might a *memory bank* look like?
What could it do?
What types of banks exist?

Responses included:

- River bank
- Blood bank
- Organ bank for spare parts
- Money bank
- Memory bank.

Then the idea of a bank where your memories could be kept safe was explored.

Who might use this bank?
Why?
Would anyone try to rob it?
Why?

Ideas were listed on the board.

Rough Drafts

Second, written drafts of playscripts were attempted. Decisions were made on working titles, the characters and the plot.

The title 'Memory Bank Robbers' was chosen early because it tells what the play is about and hints at conflict through the word *robbers*.

To choose the cast, these questions were answered:

- Who works in a bank?
- Who visits a bank?
- Who might defend the bank?

One of the responses was *Thought Guards*. Since they are defending feelings or ideas, they don't need guns. What could they use for protection? Torches? Brain wavers (stack helmets)?

Props were discussed and suggestions included 'A Memory Lane' sign; clocks or watches for the Time Robbers; a mirror for one-way deposits.

Then students discussed whether sound effects or music would be needed; computer beeps? dog barks?

The setting – could the bank be shown by a sign? If so, what, kind? A big M? Or would that look too much like McDonalds hamburgers?

Workshopping

On a reading, there seemed to be little humour in the script, so the character of the Watch Dog was introduced. Some parts were too long so an Assistant took half of the Manager's speeches and the Teller became No.1 Teller and No.2 Teller.

This was an 'ideas' play but still needed some action.

Could the Time Robbers be stopped by the Thought Guards?

How could this be shown without violence?

Was the major idea being explored obvious to the audience? The stress was on the words, so perhaps it would have made a better radio play?

When it was acted, with one student timing the performance at 20 minutes, it was thought to be too long. Students decided where the words needed to be cut.

The Face Tree

A classroom performance and discussion script about coping with feelings of loss, for primary school students.

Cast

(minimum of 11, maximum of 30)

- JO, a boy or girl who recently lost someone or something important
- GUIDE
- X, the person who has left or died
- FACES CHORUSES (each chorus consists of 1–5 students who make and wear appropriate face masks)
- SAD CHORUS
- MAD CHORUS
- GLAD CHORUS
- LONELY CHORUS
- FEARFUL CHORUS
- CRYBABY CHORUS (with tissues box)
- CUDDLE CHORUS (with big arms)
- GUILTY CHORUS
- SMILING CHORUS

Props

- Face Tree: Hat-stand with hooks for branches holding 'faces' (masks from paper plates)
- Box of tissues
- Hose
- Lightweight blocks for building (5–10)
- Soft toy for throwing

Setting

- The People Garden

The Face Tree

GUIDE	This is the People Garden. Here is the Face Tree.
JO	(*walking around tree*) I've never seen a tree like this before.
GUIDE	Most trees have leaves. The Face Tree has faces.
JO	(*touching masks*) May I play with these?
GUIDE	If you need them.
JO	How do I play?
GUIDE	It's like picking flowers. Choose any face masks you need.
CHORUSES	(*bow*) We are the masks!
GUIDE	Recently, someone important left you.
JO	Yes.
GUIDE	It's okay to show how you feel.
JO	I feel sad.
GUIDE	You wish that X didn't leave. But you couldn't stop them. So you feel sad.
JO	Yes.
GUIDE	Choose a Sad Face.
JO	Okay. (*walks around tree*) Which one is really Sad?
SAD CHORUS	(*form a line and bow*) We are the Sad Faces. This is how we look. (*shows*) Do you need one of us now?

JO	I'm not sure. But I'm glad to know you're there.
GUIDE	Can you show me a sad face? (*JO tries to copy sad faces. They touch JO's face, trying to make the mouth turn down more.*)
SAD CHORUS	Make your mouth turn down.
JO	I feel sad about losing X. (*Sad Faces gather around, nodding.*)
SAD CHORUS	We know how you feel. We cry a lot. (*tears*)
JO	(*crossly*) I'm not a Crybaby.
CRYBABY CHORUS	(*crying loudly*) We're the Crybaby Chorus. We cry a lot. Boo Hoo Boo Hoo. (*Give JO a box of tissues*) Here. Help yourself. It's okay to be like us, Sometimes.
JO	(*hesitantly takes tissue, sniffs*) Thanks.
SAD CHORUS	There's nothing wrong with crying. We cry a lot. In the shower, where no-one can hear, Or in bed, Crying makes us feel better. Of course, you don't want this much water around! (*spray with hose for tears*)
JO	I tried crying in the shower. That's okay.
CRYBABY CHORUS	We like to cry with someone. It helps both of us. (*cry on each others' shoulders*)
GUIDE	(*jumping out of the way*) I'm getting wet!
SAD CHORUS	(*winding up hose and putting it away*) Sorry.
GUIDE	There are other faces.

JO	(*touching tree*) This is a Lonely Face. (*Lonely Faces make a circle around JO*)
LONELY CHORUS	We are the Lonely Faces. We feel left out. We feel left behind.
JO	I feel like that. Sometimes.
GUIDE	That's okay. If you've lost someone important, You do feel left behind. You do feel lonely. (*LONELY CHORUS bow and leave*)
JO	(*alarmed*) They're leaving! Don't they need to talk?
LONELY CHORUS	Yes. We're going to tell our friends how we feel. (*LONELY CHORUS chat to others*)
JO	Don't you want to talk to me?
LONELY CHORUS	Want one of our masks?
JO	Thanks.
LONELY CHORUS	Now we feel a bit better. (*hang faces back on tree*)
JO	I'm glad.
GLAD CHORUS	(*racing across*) Glad! Did you call us? We're the Glad Faces.
JO	No. Not yet.
FEARFUL CHORUS	We are the Fearful Faces. Do you feel scared?
JO	Sometimes. I'm afraid that someone else will leave too. I'm afraid that ... (*fill in something*) I'm afraid of a lot of things.

FEARFUL CHORUS	We know how you feel. Call if you need us.
JO	Thanks.
GUIDE	Over here are the Mad Faces.
MAD CHORUS	(*storming up and down, stamping feet*) We are the Mad Faces. Do you need us?
JO	(*stamping feet*) Yes. I do feel mad. Why did X have to leave? It isn't fair!
GUIDE	No it isn't fair. But it wasn't your fault X left.
GUILTY CHORUS	(*creeping across*) We are the Guilty Chorus. We feel bad. We think it was our fault.
JO	Was it my fault that X left? Did I do something wrong? If I had been good, would s/he have stayed?
GUIDE	Sometimes, we feel guilty. But often it's not our fault. The bad thing just happened. We didn't cause it.
MAD CHORUS	But it isn't fair! It makes us mad! (*throwing things*)
GUIDE	Jo, what do you most feel like doing, when you're mad?
JO	(*picks up soft toy but doesn't throw it*) I've never felt this mad before.
MAD CHORUS	Do you feel like throwing things?

JO	Sometimes.
MAD CHORUS	Do you feel like shouting?
JO	(*shouting*) Sometimes.
MAD CHORUS	Try this. (*offers collection of blocks*) Stack these blocks. Each time you add a block, say something which is unfair, It's not fair when ...
JO	(*adds block*) people I like go away.
MAD CHORUS	It's not fair when ... (*add one or two examples*)
GUIDE	Jo, I'll tell you something fun to do. Knock down those things which make you feel mad.
JO	(*knocks down block tower*) Great!
MAD CHORUS	(*collecting blocks*) You don't need us any more.
CUDDLE CHORUS	(*stretching out arms*) We're Cuddles. Do you want us?
JO	Yes. Sometimes. (*they cuddle JO who cuddles back*)
SMILING CHORUS	We're the Smiling Faces. Do you want us?
JO	Sometimes.
GUIDE	Are there any other faces you need?
JO	Maybe. Perhaps a Hiding Face. I'll let you know.
GUIDE	Which face would you like to take home? (*FACES CHORUS gather masks from tree and hang them all on JO, or link hands surrounding JO*)

JO

I can feel sad about X leaving.
(*SAD CHORUS bow*)
I can feel mad.
(*MAD CHORUS bow*)
Sometimes I might feel lonely.
(*LONELY CHORUS bow*)
Or want to hide. I feel afraid that more bad things might happen.
(*FEARFUL CHORUS bow*)
But I don't need to feel guilty.
(*GUILTY CHORUS nod*)
Sometimes I might feel like a cuddle.
(CUDDLE CHORUS *wrap arms around each other*)
But underneath, I'm still Jo.

JO

(*touching trunk*) If this tree grows faces, what are the roots like?

GUIDE

You'll have to find out! Next time you visit the People Garden, new masks might be on the Face Tree. Or you might not need to wear a mask. It's okay to show how you feel without using a mask.

JO

I feel ... a bit better now.

Extension Activities

Faces

With your hand, demonstrate wiping all expression from your face.

"Copy me.
Put on a happy-face mask.
Now wipe it off.
Put on a face mask that is sad/scared etc.
Wipe it off.
Tell me some other faces.
Show me some other faces.
Let's copy your face.
Is it hard to tell the difference between a scared and a hiding face?"

Discuss the difficulty of distinguishing between different faces. Use this discussion as a preliminary to making masks.

Making Masks

Using paper plates and texta colours, design masks for the following feelings:

- Sad
- Glad
- Mad
- Hiding
- Fear
- Lonely
- Smiling, etc.

Make a tree upon which to hang the masks. Use a broom, a hatstand, bag hooks or whatever is available.

Discussion

If the Face Tree grows masks, what will the roots look like?

Little masks? Feet? Shoes? What will the buds look like?

Will the tree need to be watered? With what? Will the tree need to be fed? How?

What happens to the tree during a storm?

Where might the tree be planted? In Autumn, might the tree lose its masks? Who might pick the faces?

How might they be used?

What about a Sunny Shop (like a florist) selling bunches or arrangements of Sunny Masks?

Why might people use masks?

When might it be okay to take them off?

Where is Miss Caterpillar?

A classroom script about change for junior students. An alternative title could be 'Where is Mr Caterpillar?'

Cast

- STORYTELLER (can be read by teacher)
- MISS CATERPILLAR
- COCOON
- MISS BUTTERFLY

Chorus

- SEED
- BIRDS
- BEES
- TREES
- WIND
- RAIN
- SUN
- FLOWERS
- BUTTERFLIES (any number)

Costumes

- Simple outfits such as brown pants and green tops for trees, can be made. Cut cellophane paper and drape from arms for leaves, sun rays or flower stems.
- Flowers can use paper plate shapes on sticks, or their hands to form flower faces.

Setting

- The bush

Where is Miss Caterpillar?

STORYTELLER	This is the Bush. I am the Storyteller. My story is about Trees.
CHORUS	(*rushing in*) Where is Miss Caterpillar?
STORYTELLER	The Trees might have seen her. These are the Trees.
TREES	(*bow*) We are the Trees.
CHORUS	Have you seen Miss Caterpillar?
TREES	Not today. Ask the birds.
BIRDS	We are the birds. We see everything.
CHORUS	Have you seen Miss Caterpillar?
BIRDS	No. (*swoop down and pick up something*)
STORYTELLER	Once upon a time, there was a seed. It fell on the ground. The Sun shone.
SUN	I am the Sun. I shine.
STORYTELLER	And the Wind blew.
WIND	I am the Wind. I blow.
STORYTELLER	And the Rain fell.
RAIN	I am the Rain. I fall. Drip. Drip. Drip.

STORYTELLER	The seed began to grow.
	It grew shoots.
	It grew leaves.
	It grew into a big tree.
	Then the birds came.
BIRDS	(*fly and sit on trees*)
	We sit on trees.
FLOWERS	(*sit around tree*)
	We are the flowers.
	We grow under the tree.
STORYTELLER	Someone nibbled at the leaves.
CHORUS	(*loudly*) Miss Caterpillar?
STORYTELLER	Yes.
	Miss Caterpillar ate so much.
	She grew and grew.
BIRDS	(*flying around tree*)
	Let's have a snack. Let's eat that!
STORYTELLER	Miss Caterpillar hid under the branches. She was sleepy.
CHORUS	What happened next?
STORYTELLER	Miss Caterpillar got lost. In the Bush, the Sun shone.
SUN	I am the Sun. I shine.
STORYTELLER	And the Wind blew.
WIND	I am the Wind. I blow.
STORYTELLER	And the Rain fell.
RAIN	I am the Rain.
	I fall. Drip. Drip. Drip.

TREES	We are the trees. We give shade. We hide things in our branches.
COCOON	I hide in the branches. I'm a cocoon. I have a case outside me. I'm sleepy.
STORYTELLER	When you wake up, you'll feel different.
COCOON	(*crossly*) No I won't! Let me go back to sleep.
CHORUS	Where is Miss Caterpillar?
SUN	I can't see Miss Caterpillar.
WIND	I can't see Miss Caterpillar.
STORYTELLER	In the Bush, many things change. They are not lost, They become something else.
CHORUS	We've been looking for ages. Where is Miss Caterpillar? Is she dead? Did the birds eat her?
BIRDS	We couldn't find her.
STORYTELLER	Miss Caterpillar isn't dead, She's just changing.
CHORUS	Is she changing clothes?
STORYTELLER	She is changing her shape. Here comes Miss Butterfly.
MISS BUTTERFLY	I am Miss Butterfly.
CHORUS	Where did you come from?
MISS BUTTERFLY	A cocoon.
CHORUS	And before that?

MISS BUTTERFLY	Long ago, I was a caterpillar.
	(*flutter past*) We are the Butterflies.
	We can fly.
	Now we are beautiful.
	We used to be caterpillars.
STORYTELLER	Once upon a time, there was a caterpillar.
	She was called Miss Caterpillar.
	She got lost.
	She changed into a cocoon.
	Then she became Miss Butterfly.
	(*each of the actors is introduced and takes a bow*)
	(*This can also be done at the beginning as a way of settling very young actors.*)

The Day Our Mouse Died

A classroom discussion script for primary students.

It's likely that a pet will die, either at home, or in the classroom if the school has pets.

'The Day Our Mouse Died' script deals with ways of handling this. Rehearsals give opportunities to discuss whether to have a ritual and/or replace the pet.

Many educators race out to find look-a-likes to replace the original pet, but current grief counselling suggests acknowledging the death is part of the grieving process, regardless of spiritual or religious beliefs. A script is a good way to enable indirect discussion.

If a student's pet at home has died, they can use some of the earlier activities for acknowledging their feelings.

Cast

- NARRATOR
- TEACHER
- BEN
- TRAVERS
- ANNA
- SAMANTHA, who plays the recorder
- ANDY
- MOUSE
- CARETAKER, Mr Smith
- STUDENT CHORUS

Props

- Broom
- Mouse
- Cardboard box
- Mouse box

- Recorder
- Mouse bell
- Flowers

Setting

- A classroom

The Day Our Mouse Died

CARETAKER	(*sweeps floor in classroom, stops at mouse box, notices mouse is dead*) Oh no! The students will be upset. I wonder if I've got time to get to the pet shop and back! (*races out of room*)
NARRATOR	The class had a pet mouse. Mo was her name. The mouse lived in a box. The students took turns looking after Mo. (*Students enter classroom and gather around mouse box*)
TRAVERS	Mo looks different.
STUDENT CHORUS	What's wrong with Mo?
TEACHER	(*walks into room*) Good morning class.
BEN	There's something wrong with Mo.
TEACHER	(*looks at mouse, sadly*) Yes. I think Mo is dead.
TRAVERS	She isn't moving.
ANNA	She's lying on her back.

BEN	What's wrong with Mo? Take her out.
ANNA	She feels stiff.
BEN	Is she really dead?
ANNA	I've never seen anyone dead before.
BEN	She's cold.
CARETAKER	(*returns, holding a live mouse, upset that students have found the dead Mo*) (*gently*) I've brought another mouse to replace Mo. Looks like she's gone.
BEN	Gone where?
CARETAKER	I don't know.
TEACHER	You mean that she's died.
CARETAKER	(*nods*)
ANNA	But Mo was all right yesterday. Why did she die? Was it something we did?
TRAVERS	Can't you undead Mo, like a replay on TV?
TEACHER	No Travers. This is real.
CARETAKER	It's dead. I'll get rid of it.
ANNA	Mo wasn't an 'it'. Mo was part of our class. She used to squeak and drop on me. When I was mouse minder, she climbed through my hair.
TEACHER	We must say 'goodbye' to Mo. We must have a funeral for Mo. This morning.
ANNA	What's a funeral?

TEACHER	It's a special time to say 'goodbye'. We talk about the person who has died. We talk about the good things we did together. We might cry. That's okay.
TRAVERS	What happens to the body?
TEACHER	Usually the dead person is buried in the ground. Or the body is burnt. But first the body is put into a coffin.
TRAVERS	Is that a box?
BEN	Will my lunch box do?
TRAVERS	Yuk!
TEACHER	Usually a coffin is a wooden box.
BEN	Would a cardboard one do?
TEACHER	Is there anything special about Mo that you want to put in the coffin with her?
ANNA	Her bell. She liked playing with the bell in her box.
SAMANTHA	I'll play my recorder. Mo liked music.
BEN	But not yours.
TRAVERS	Mo was used to Samantha practising.
SAMANTHA	(*plays the recorder*)
TEACHER	A funeral is a time to talk about your memories of the person. Let's take it in turns. What do you remember, Ben?
BEN	I remember when Mo got her name. We had a competition.
STUDENT CHORUS	There were lots of names. But then we said eenie, meany, minni, mo.

TRAVERS	We didn't want to call her Meany.
	Mo was the best one.
ANNA	I remember when Mo got out.
	We chased her around the principal's office.
TRAVERS	I remember when Mo dropped a blob on Andy's maths.
ANDY	I didn't mind. I don't like maths.
TEACHER	Sometimes people write poems about a person who has died. Perhaps we could do that this morning. And then read the poems when we bury Mo.
BEN	Where will we bury Mo?
TRAVERS	In the dump bin?
ANDY	No! What about under the big tree?
	Near the school rose-garden.
STUDENT CHORUS	Then Mo will hear the birds.
ANDY	You can't hear anything when you're dead.
TRAVERS	How do you know?
TEACHER	We don't.
CARETAKER	I'll pick a few flowers from the garden.
	Almost all funerals have flowers.
ANDY	I'd like to put some flowers on Mo's grave.
TEACHER	Anna is good at making things, perhaps she could make a marker to go on the grave. With Mo's name on it.
ANNA	All right.
BEN	Do we put when Mo died on the marker?

TEACHER	Often people write special messages.
	And they put the date of birth and when the person died.
	(*Students prepare flowers, poems and cardboard box for Mo. SAMANTHA plays music; they carry box out.*)
NARRATOR	Mr Smith, the caretaker put the new mouse into Mo's old box.
CARETAKER	I thought you might like to name this mouse?
TEACHER	Soon we will, but not today.
STUDENT CHORUS	It's not the same.
	Mo was special.
	We'll never forget Mo.
CARETAKER	Until you're ready, I'll call the mouse Wait-a-Bit.

The Memory Bank Robbers

A playscript about handling memories for primary classroom discussion and performance.

Running time 12–15 minutes

Cast

(minimum of 12, maximum of 30)

- NO. 1 TELLER
- NO. 2 TELLER
- NEW CUSTOMER
- OLD MAN WITH PHOTOGRAPHS
- CUSTOMER'S CHORUS (any number)
- BANK MANAGER
- ASSISTANT MANAGER
- MEMORIES (any number) with dog leads and masks, including sad cat (losing a pet) memory and happy (beach holiday) memory.
- TIME ROBBERS (any number) wearing stop watches, clocks and calendars.
- WATCH-DOG who helps look after the bank. (Non-speaking part)
- SCIENTIST with stained, white coat and badge saying DR CHEM.
- THOUGHT GUARDS (any number,) who use their minds, not guns. They may use telepathy or mindwaves and wear stack hats called 'brain wavers'.
- SFX computer noises, e.g. Beep. Beep. Beep.

Props

- Sign 'Corner of Brain and Memory Lane'
- Sign 'Memory Bank' (perhaps in an M shape?)
- Bank cards and passbook
- Dog leads for Memories
- Teller's desk

- Computer
- Family photograph album
- Diary
- Stopwatch, clocks and calendars for Time Robbers
- Mirror
- Brain wavers, like stack hat safety helmets and torches
- Thinking cap
- Torches

Setting

- The Memory Bank, at the corner of Brain and Memory Lane

Ideas for Script Extension

- Only depositors can see details of the account through the memory bank mirror. Others see only their reflection in the mirror.
- Bank Robbers could include:
  - people who have lost their memories
  - unhappy people who want to swap bad for good memories
  - Recyclers – making bad into good memories
  - Memory Witch to make a spell from bad feelings.
- The Memory bank is kept within a watch. The depositor's code is entered through the second hand or the screen.
- A pencil contains the Memory Bank. Depositors break the lead and write their memory choices.

The Memory Bank Robbers

NO. 1 TELLER	Good morning. May I help you?
NEW CUSTOMER	Is this the bank?
NO. 2 TELLER	Which bank do you want? There are lots of different types of banks.
CHORUS	Do you want the Blood Bank?
NEW CUSTOMER	No.
CHORUS	Do you want the River Bank?
NEW CUSTOMER	No.
CHORUS	Do you want the Money Bank?
NEW CUSTOMER	No. I want the bank where I deposit my memories.
NO. 1 TELLER	You've come to the right place. This is the Memory Bank. We keep memories here.
NEW CUSTOMER	I want to open an account.
NO. 2 TELLER	What do you want to deposit?
NEW CUSTOMER	Some happy memories.
NO. 1 TELLER	Here is the bank manager.
NO. 2 TELLER	The manager will help you.
BANK MANAGER	I am the bank manager. People put memories into my bank for safe keeping. Sometimes, they take out memories.
ASSISTANT	Do you have any memories to deposit?
NEW CUSTOMER	Yes. I'd like to deposit my best holiday memory. (*pulls Memory forward on lead*)
BANK MANAGER	(*taking lead*) Is this a happy memory?

NEW CUSTOMER	Yes.
ASSISTANT	Sometimes people deposit sad memories.
CHORUS	(*walking across with SAD CAT MEMORY on lead*) When our cat died, we put our sad feelings into the Memory Bank.
NO. 1 TELLER	(*accepts memory; starts writing details*)
BANK MANAGER	Memories can be ideas, things you've been given, or feelings.
ASSISTANT	Our Memory Bank offers many services.
NEW CUSTOMER	What kind of services?
BANK MANAGER	Memory Express Cards. (*shows an Express Card*)
BANK MANAGER	We call them ME cards.
ASSISTANT	M for Memory. E for Express.
BANK MANAGER	You can put in or take out.
NEW CUSTOMER	Take out what?
BANK MANAGER	Memories. When you need them.
ASSISTANT	Put them in when you're young. Take them out when you're older.
BANK MANAGER	Feelings attract high interest around here. Even sad ones.
NEW CUSTOMER	(*looking around*) How will I know which memories are mine? It could be a lucky dip.
NO. 1 TELLER	We give you a Memory Passbook. (*shows a bank passbook*)
NO. 2 TELLER	And you have your own number. Deposit at any time.

WATCH DOG	(*wags tail*)
BANK MANAGER	Our Watch Dogs look after memories. Press their dog tags and your memories will be transferred to our bank.
NO. 2 TELLER	(*crossly*) Automatic Dog tellers are not as good as us.
WATCH DOG	Woof. Woof.
NO. 1 TELLER	Watch Dogs won't look after any good memories about cats. They just lose them.
WATCH DOG	Woof. Woof.
BANK MANAGER	Get back to work. You have another customer.
NO. 2 TELLER	Good morning sir.
OLD MAN WITH PHOTOGRAPHS	
	(*fiddling with family photo album*) Sometimes, I forget numbers or faces. So I want to put my memories into the bank, for safe keeping, in case I forget them.
BANK MANAGER	But you can also put in nice things you remember about people, or places or things.
ASSISTANT	I can arrange for you to invest.
BANK MANAGER	Do you want a high interest rate? Or do you want your memories to be safe?
OLD MAN WITH PHOTOGRAPHS	
	How will I remember, if my memories are in here?
NO. 1 TELLER	(*putting them into computer*) Your memories are safe with us.

SFX	Beep. Beep. Beep.
NO. 2 TELLER	You don't want them to be damaged by old age or forgetfulness.
ASSISTANT	We keep them in alphabetical order.
NEW CUSTOMER	(*hands over diary*) I keep some of my memories in here.
NO. 1 TELLER	Thank you. Here is a Memory Pass Book. Is this a private memory or a public one?
NEW CUSTOMER	What do you mean?
BANK MANAGER	Do you want to keep your memory secret, or do you want to share your feelings or ideas? Like this scientist.
SCIENTIST	(*stomps across*) I am Dr Chem. I am a scientist. I have worked out my dream of how to get world peace.
NO. 1 TELLER	Is this a private or public dream?
SCIENTIST	Public. If you dream alone, it is only a dream. If you dream together, it is the beginning of reality.
NO. 2 TELLER	(*puzzled about where to store it*) Is that an idea, a memory or a dream?
SCIENTIST	It's just an old saying. Maybe it's a dream.
ASSISTANT	Do you want other people to share your peace memory?
SCIENTIST	Yes.
NO. 1 TELLER	Okay. World Peace is stored under public.
SCIENTIST	Thank you.

BANK MANAGER	We remember everything here.
NO. 1 TELLER	Having fun at parties.
NO. 2 TELLER	Feeling sad about losing a pet.
NO. 1 TELLER	Doing silly things with friends who have now left.
NO. 2 TELLER	Our friends who have died. We still remember them.
ASSISTANT	Even brain waves can be stored in our Memory Bank.
NO. 1 TELLER	(*to NEW CUSTOMER*) Here is a safety deposit box. This is your key.
NO. 2 TELLER	Put anything you like inside. We will not look.
BANK MANAGER	Lock up your private memories. Public memories we keep over there. (*points to a mirror*) Stand over there. Put on the thinking cap. Think about the memories you want to share with others. The mirror will look after them. (*While NEW CUSTOMER is putting on cap near mirror, ROBBERS run in noisily*)
NEW CUSTOMER	(*frightened*) Who are they?
ROBBERS	(*wearing stop watches, clocks and calendars*) Put your hands up. This is a bank robbery.
ROBBER	(*run across. They use a stop watch*) Stop! We are the Memory Bank Robbers!
BANK MANAGER	What do you want?
ROBBERS	We want to steal your best memories.
CUSTOMER'S CHORUS	
	(*putting up hands*) Why?

ROBBERS	We are the time robbers.
BANK MANAGER	These memories belong to our customers. You can't have them. Who are you working for?
ROBBERS	Old Father Time. He collects what others forget.
NEW CUSTOMER	Why doesn't he leave the memories in the bank? They belong to the depositors.
ROBBERS	Hand over your favourite memory ... or else!
OLD MAN WITH PHOTOGRAPHS	Which one? I've lost my memory. Will you help me find it ?
ROBBERS	Where did you leave your memory? Do you have any ID?
OLD MAN	What's that?
SCIENTIST	Identity. Something which says who you are (*points to his badge*) I'm Dr Chem.
OLD MAN	I'm not sure. (*THOUGHT GUARDS run in and stop ROBBERS by beaming their thoughts perhaps with torches-WATCH DOG helps wind his lead around ROBBERS*)
WATCH DOG	Woof. Woof. Woof.
GUARDS	Stop! We are the Thought Guards. Come with us. To the Memory Lane police station.
ROBBERS	No.

THOUGHT GUARDS	Oh yes you will. People deserve to have their memories protected. They don't want to lose them to people like you. (*marches ROBBERS away*)
NEW CUSTOMER	Who would want to steal from a Memory Bank?
BANK MANAGER	Old Father Time. He steals memories from everybody.
SCIENTIST	I wish they'd taken my world peace idea.
NO. 1 TELLER	They wouldn't know what to do with it.
NEW CUSTOMER	I'm glad my memories are safe in your bank.
BANK MANAGER	Our Thought Guards are very good.
THOUGHT GUARDS	(*bow*) Thank you.
WATCH DOG	Woof. Woof. Woof.
OLD MAN	(*happily patting dog*) I remember that watch dog. I'm not memoryrupt.
CUSTOMER'S CHORUS	Where else can we leave our memories?
BANK MANAGER	Outside, we have automatic tellers. Anytime you want to visit your memories. Just use this Memory Express card.
ASSISTANT	Or use an email. You can bank online. We're very up to date.
BANK MANAGER	We keep your memories in alphabetical order.
CUSTOMER'S CHORUS	Just like a directory!

ASSISTANT	Key in your feelings and we will find your memories.
	A is for Angry
	B is for ...
	C is for ...
	And we go right through to Z.
SCIENTIST	What's Z?
BANK MANAGER	That memory is secret!
	And in the Memory Bank, we keep secrets.

Sadako and the Thousand Cranes

There is a Japanese belief that if a sick person folds one thousand paper cranes, the gods will grant their wish and make the person well again.

Sadako Sasaki was two years old when the atom bomb was dropped on the Japanese city of Hiroshima in 1945. Ten years later, she became sick from the radiation and developed leukemia. While in hospital, she began folding paper cranes and had completed 644 cranes which hung around her bed.

Her classmates folded the rest for her.

Now in the Hiroshima Peace Park there is a memorial to her, and children leave folded cranes that they have made in her honour.

Peace Day is held on August sixth. It is in memory of those who died when the atom bomb was dropped.

On Peace Day, children around the world, now make paper cranes.

Cast

- SADAKO
- CHIZUKO, her friend NURSE
- MOTHER
- FATHER
- 1ST CRANE (gold paper)
- 2ND CRANE
- 3RD CRANE
- CHORUS OF PAPER CRANES (any number of students)
- CLASSMATES
- NARRATOR

Props

- Bed
- Gold paper

- Paper to make cranes
- Kokeshi, the doll
- Book of Sadako's story

Setting

- Hospital

Sadako and the Thousand Cranes

NURSE	How are you feeling today Sadako?
SADAKO	Better.
NURSE	Do you still feel dizzy?
SADAKO	Sometimes. Do I have the atom bomb disease?
NURSE	The doctors are making tests.
SADAKO	Sometimes I feel weak.
NURSE	Your friend has come to visit. She has brought you a present.
CHIZUKO	Hi Sadako. I've got something for you.
SADAKO	Here's something for you too. I wrote a letter to my classmates. Will you take it for me?
CHIZUKO	Yes. Now look at this.
SADAKO	It's just a piece of gold paper.
CHIZUKO	But when it is folded ... (*1ST CRANE twists into shape*)

SADAKO	It's a crane! (*CRANE nods and folds wings*)
CHIZUKO	It is said that if you fold one thousand cranes ...
SADAKO	One thousand!
CHIZUKO	If you fold one thousand paper cranes, the gods will grant your wish ...
SADAKO	I wish that I could be well again.
CHIZUKO	This is the first crane. Here is some paper for the second one. How many more?
SADAKO	Only 998 to go.
CHIZUKO	You're better than me at adding up.
NURSE	Time to go now. Sadako must rest.
CHIZUKO	I'll bring you more paper next time.
SADAKO	Thanks.
NURSE	I'll hang up your crane. Go to sleep now. Your parents will visit soon. (*NURSE tidies bed, SADAKO sleeps and NURSE arranges cranes, then leaves*)
CRANE CHORUS	(*dancing gracefully*) We are the paper cranes. Look how beautifully we are folded. Look at our wings. We can fly anywhere. We have come from the past. We can fly into the future. (*SADAKO wakes up, watches the CRANES and smiles. PARENTS arrive. CRANES freeze*)
MOTHER	We heard about your cranes. Here is some paper for you Sadako.
SADAKO	Thank you. Look at my cranes hanging from the roof. (*CRANES frozen as if hanging from roof*)

FATHER	I've saved some paper for you.
SADAKO	I wish my sickness was over. I want to go home.
FATHER	We must wait for the doctors' tests.
SADAKO	But they do so many tests.
FATHER	How many cranes have you folded now?
SADAKO	I'm not sure.
FATHER	Let's count them.
CRANES	(*each steps forward to say own number*)
CHORUS	One, two, three ... Fifty-five ...
FATHER	So many.
SADAKO	And so many more to fold.
CRANES CHORUS	We are the paper cranes. Look how beautifully we are folded. Look at our wings. We can fly anywhere. We have come from the past. We can fly into the future.
NURSE	Go to sleep now Sadako. Time to rest.
CLASSMATES	We've brought a present for you.
SADAKO	More paper?
CLASSMATES	And something else. This is Kokeshi.
SADAKO	A doll!
CLASSMATES	To stay with you, while you are in hospital.
SADAKO	(*hugs doll*) Thank you.
NURSE	Time to go now. Sadako must rest.
SADAKO	So must Kokeshi.

NURSE	Yes.
	(*SADAKO sleeps. Her PARENTS visit and kiss her goodbye. Then NURSE checks*)
CHIZUKO	Sadako folded six hundred and forty-four cranes.
CLASSMATES	She didn't finish in time. We will fold the others for her.
CHIZUKO	How many more? I'm not good at maths.
CLASSMATES	Three hundred and fifty-six. We will fold them for her.
FATHER	Our daughter has gone. But we still remember her.
MOTHER	Our daughter has gone. But everybody remembers. One thousand paper cranes were buried with her.
CLASSMATES	After the funeral, we collected all of Sadako's letters. We published them in a book.
NARRATOR	It was called Kokeshi after the doll we gave her in the hospital. The book was sent around Japan.
CLASSMATES	This is Sadako's Memorial. It is in the Hiroshima Peace Park. On August sixth, it is Peace day. Children from all over the world fold paper cranes. They leave them for Peace.
CRANES CHORUS	We are the paper cranes. Look how beautifully we are folded. Look at our wings. We can fly anywhere. We have come from the past. We can fly into the future.

Nursery Rhymes Ltd

A playscript about losing a friend. This script is incomplete and allows students to take the play in the direction they want.

Cast

(minimum of 12, maximum of 30)

- HUMPTY DUMPTY, with a bandage on his head
- MR ASK ME (could be a computer)
- QUEEN OF HEARTS
- BO PEEP
- MARY
- BOY BLUE
- MOTHER HUBBARD
- DOG, of Mother Hubbard
- MISS MUFFET
- JACK AND JILL
- CHILD
- CARETAKER, of Lost and Found Department
- LOST SHEEP (any number)
- CATS (any number) from any nursery rhymes, e.g. Pussy in the Well
- MICE (any number) from any nursery rhymes, e.g. Three Blind Mice
- KING'S HORSES (any number)
- KING'S MEN (any number)
- GIRL WITH A CURL

Props

- Information desk

Setting

- Lost and Found Department of Nursery Rhymes Ltd

Nursery Rhymes Ltd

HUMPTY DUMPTY	(*holding head*) Excuse me.
MR ASK ME	Can I help you? I'm Mr Ask Me. People ask me things.
HUMPTY DUMPTY	My name is Humpty Dumpty. I want to find the Lost Department.
MR ASK ME	What have you lost?
HUMPTY DUMPTY	I can't remember. I fell off a wall.
MR ASK ME	Try the third floor. Our Lost and Found Department is there. (*Nursery rhyme characters arrive*)
MR ASK ME	Can I help you?
ALL	(*together*) Yes please.
MR ASK ME	Where do you come from?
ALL	Nursery Rhymes.
MR ASK ME	What are you looking for?
ALL	The Lost and Found Department.
MR ASK ME	Have you lost something?
ALL	Yes.
QUEEN OF HEARTS	I'm the Queen of Hearts. I've lost my tarts.
BO PEEP	I'm Little Bo Peep. I've lost my sheep. Do you know where to find them?

MR ASK ME	Try the third floor.
MARY	My name is Mary. I've lost my little lamb whose fleece was white as snow.
BOY BLUE	(*yawning*) I'm Little Boy Blue. I fell asleep, and I've lost my sheep.
MR ASK ME	Not more lost sheep! Try the third floor.
MOTHER HUBBARD	I'm Mother Hubbard. I went to the cupboard. And my dog's bone is missing.
MR ASK ME	Try the meat department.
MISS MUFFETT	I'm Little Miss Muffett. I sat on my tuffet Eating my curds and whey. Along came a spider And sat down beside me, And frightened me right away.
MR ASK ME	We don't sell curds and whey, but we sell yoghurt in the Food Hall.
MISS MUFFETT	Thank you.
JACK AND JILL	We're Jack and Jill. We climbed up the hill. But we've spilt the water!
MR ASK ME	There's a tap on the third floor.
CHILD	My name is ... (*fill in actor's real name*). I've lost my friend.
MR ASK ME	We all need friends. Try the Lost Department. They find most things. (*Everybody mimes walking stairs to third floor*)
ALL	Puff. Puff. Puff.

CARETAKER	Hello. I'm the Caretaker.
	This is the Lost and Found Department. I look after things which are lost.
	Until the owners are found.
CHILD	I lost my friend.
CARETAKER	Where did you lose them?
CHILD	At school.
QUEEN OF HEARTS	Did you have a fight?
CHILD	No.
BOY BLUE	Did he change classes?
CHILD	No.
MARY	Did he move schools?
CHILD	No.
HUMPTY	Did he move away?
CHILD	No.
BO PEEP	Did he die?
CHILD	No.
	He's just lost.
CARETAKER	These cats and mice belong in nursery rhymes.
	I wish someone would collect them.
CATS	Miaow. Miaow. Miaow.
MICE	Squeak. Squeak. Squeak.
MARY	I had a little lamb.
	Its fleece was white as snow.
	Everywhere that I went, the lamb was sure to go.
	But now I've lost it.
CARETAKER	Here are some sheep I found.

SHEEP	Baa. Baa. Baa.
CARETAKER	Here is a bone.
DOG	Woof.
QUEEN OF HEARTS	What about my lost tarts?
CARETAKER	Here are your tarts. The Knave of Hearts found them.
QUEEN OF HEARTS	Thank you.
SHEEP	Baa. Baa. Baa.
BO PEEP	(*shakes head*) Leave them alone. They'll come home And bring their tails behind them.
CARETAKER	Humpty Dumpty had a big fall. He fell off the wall.
KING'S HORSES	(*galloping on*) We're the King's horses.
KING'S MEN	(*together*) We're the King's men. We've come to put Humpty together again.
CARETAKER	I'm so glad. The fall on his head made him lose his memory.
KING'S MEN	(*helping HUMPTY off*) We'll look after him.
CHILD	Have you seen my friend?
CARETAKER	What does your friend look like?
CHILD	I'll draw my friend. (*draws*)

CARETAKER   There was a little girl,
                   Who had a little curl,
                   Right in the middle of her forehead.
                   When she was good, she was very very good
                   And when she was bad, she was horrid. Was she
                   your friend?

CHILD   No. My friend isn't horrid.

Suggest an ending to this script.

Discuss making and losing friendships.

Why do people say *lost* when they mean *dead*?

How might you *lose* a friendship?

Antarctic Dad

Loss is experienced by many. Families have parents who work away from home for long periods or who are confined elsewhere.

The book, *Antarctic Dad* by Hazel Edwards, inspired this script.

Cast

- NARRATOR
- SCHOOL KIDS CHORUS (any number) including
  - 1st SCHOOL KID
  - 2nd SCHOOL KID
  - 3rd SCHOOL KID
- DAD
- MUM
- BRAD
- DAD 1 and DAD 2
- TEACHER
- ALBATROSS couple
- GOODBYE CHORUS
- WILDLIFE CHORUS
- WAVES GYMNASTS
- ICEBERGS
- HELICOPTERS
- SHED CHORUS

Props

- Roo the soft toy (or can be a non-speaking student actor)
- Antarctic photos (postcard size and/or projected on wall)
- Map of Antarctica
- Furry hat and backpack for Dad
- Camera
- Streamers, including red
- Big book *Antarctic Dad* (can be scanned and enlarged) and used by Narrator

- Birthday cake in the shape of Antarctica (optional)
- SFX waves sound effect
- SFX electronic beeps for email messages

Setting

- School classroom

Antarctic Dad

SCHOOL KIDS' CHORUS
      Here's the new kid. Where's your dad?

NARRATOR   He's gone to work in Antarctica.

SCHOOL KIDS' CHORUS
      Sure.

NARRATOR   Don't you believe me?

SCHOOL KIDS' CHORUS
      Why should we?

NARRATOR   (*shows photos*)
      Look at these.

SCHOOL KIDS' CHORUS
      Icebergs. Penguins. And a bloke wearing a furry hat.

NARRATOR   My Dad.

SCHOOL KIDS' CHORUS
      You don't look much like him. He's got more clothes!

NARRATOR   Dad's working at a station at the bottom of the world.
      He's wintering in the Antarctic. But he's coming back.

1st SCHOOL KID	My dad works at the railway station.
2nd SCHOOL KID	My dad stays at home
3rd SCHOOL KID	Mike is my step dad. Mum says he's a beaut bloke.
BRAD	I've got two dads. And they're both coming to Sports Day.
NARRATOR	When's Sports Day at this school?
BRAD	Don't worry about that. I'm going to win every race. I'm first at everything.
1st SCHOOL KID	Because Brad pushes everybody else out (*ALBATROSS couple fly across stage*)
BRAD	(*menacingly*) Who says so!
2nd SCHOOL KID	Look, TWO albatross. Flying together.
3rd SCHOOL KID	Wow.
ALBATROSS	We are the Albatross. We fly over the icebergs of Antarctica. Look below. Sometimes the bergs roll over.
SFX	(*Optional Antarctic or flying music*) (*ICEBERGS move like pieces of a jigsaw, and then roll over and off the stage. ALBATROSS fly off together.*)
TEACHER	This term we'll study Antarctica. Perhaps our new student will have Antarctic photos to share?
SCHOOL KIDS' CHORUS	Cool! (*Dad strolls by holding camera, puzzled by instructions*)
NARRATOR	Dad's got a new camera, but he hasn't read how to work it yet, His photos are upside down.

DAD	Only because the ship rocks and rolls in the Southern Ocean.
SFX	Waves sound effect (*DANCERS mine*)
WAVES GYMNASTS	Up and down. Up and down. Like the Great Southern ocean, We go up and down. Rock and Roll. Rock and Roll. Yeah!
TEACHER	Don't forget, tomorrow is Sports Day.
BRAD	My parents are coming to see me run. They take excellent photos on their phones.
2nd SCHOOL KID	Is your Mum coming too Brad?
BRAD	Yeah.
3rd SCHOOL KID	Did she get married again, like mine?
BRAD	Yeah. My step-Dad's coming too. So I've got three parents coming. That's more than anyone else.
NARRATOR	I've only got one Mum.
MUM	And it's hard to do everything. I'm working, but I'll get there for the relay, and take a photo. Dad will be pleased you are taking part.
NARRATOR	Before Dad left, Mum had a good idea. (*DAD and MUM walk on, holding a large stuffed Roo*)
MUM	(*To DAD*) Take Roo in your backpack. (*DAD holds up the backpack which is smaller than the toy. Shrugs.*)
MUM	And here's the new camera.

NARRATOR	Take a photo of Roo wherever you go.
MUM	Then we'll know what it's like where you are working.
DAD	Okay. But let's take a practice shot now. (*DAD tries to take a family photo with Roo. Fools around*)
NARRATOR	It's upside down!
DAD	Lots of time to practise in Antarctica over winter.
MUM	Time to go to the wharf to say goodbye. (*GOODBYE CHORUS march on, throwing streamers to audience*)
NARRATOR	At the wharf, we waved goodbye as the polar ship left. (*Using streamers, dance mime a goodbye dance*) (*DAD throws a red streamer to the narrator, who catches it.*)
NARRATOR	Got it!
DAD	(*ties streamer to Roo's foot*) Look.
MUM	Oh no. Roo is falling in!
NARRATOR	Good catch Dad.
DAD	(*catching Roo*) Search and Rescue training is never wasted. Take a photo! Show the kids at school.
TEACHER:	Welcome to Sports Day. (*Brad's two Dads arrive. MUM runs in late*)
TEACHER	Ready Set Go. (*RUNNERS/SCHOOL KIDS CHORUS mime relay running, BRAD's team wins.*)
BRAD	Told you so.

TEACHER	There were others in your team Brad. Team work matters.
	(*NARRATOR comes last and MUM takes a photo*)
MUM	We'll send it to Dad.
NARRATOR	Dad emailed me.
SFX	Email 'beeps' noises.
DAD	Good try. Here's a picture of Roo running after a penguin.
NARRATOR	Brad thinks he knows everything.
BRAD	What's that map on the wall?
NARRATOR	(*points*) That's the station where my Dad works.
BRAD	Doesn't look like a railway station.
NARRATOR	It isn't a train station. My dad doesn't drive trains. But he does ride Zodiacs in the water and quads across the ice.
BRAD	What's that shed?
SHED CHORUS	(*holding red sign*) We're the Red Shed. That's the Red Shed where Dad sleeps and eats.
SHED CHORUS	(*twisting to green sign*) We're the Green Shed. That's the Green Shed with the stores for two years.
SHED CHORUS	(*twisting to yellow*) We're the Yellow Shed. That's the Yellow Shed for the Met reports about the weather.
HELICOPTERS	We're the helicopters ... known as the choppers We travel in pairs for safety. In a blizz, the big trucks form a circle to shelter us. Otherwise we'd be blown away. Team work matters.
BRAD	Cool! Is your dad a pilot?

NARRATOR	No, but sometimes he flies. (*DAD flies in the chopper, photographing the wildlife*)
NARRATOR	I like birds and animals. Antarctica has penguins, seals and whales. (*The penguins parade. The whales swim. The seals dive. The Albatross dance too.*)
NARRATOR	Mum likes the Albatross best.
MUM	Those birds stay together forever. Like us, we hope.
SFX	Email beeps.
NARRATOR	Dad emails me every day.
DAD	Today I saw an Emperor penguin. Mark it on our wildlife map.
NARRATOR	He gives me the co-ordinates. (*draws a red cross on wildlife map of Antarctica.*)
TEACHER	Your turn for show and tell.
NARRATOR	This is where my dad saw an Emperor.
BRAD	Is an Emperor like a king of Antarctica? (*All laugh*)
NARRATOR	Sort of. Want to see an ele seal, Brad? Bring you a photo tomorrow. Wildlife rules, okay?
BRAD	Ugly.
NARRATOR	Dad says they're huge like elephants, but the babies are called weaners. They're cute.
SFX	Beep email noises.
DAD	Email me your homework to check.

TEACHER	This week we have a project on weather in Antarctica.
SCHOOL KIDS' CHORUS	Cool.
BRAD	Antarctica isn't on the TV weather news map. I can't do that project.
NARRATOR	Check my Dad's site and the web cam. The Met guys send up balloons to check on the weather. Temperature might be as low as minus 20°C.
SCHOOL KIDS' CHORUS	Cool.
NARRATOR	It's my birthday this weekend. Usually Dad runs the party games. I miss him a lot.
MUM	I've made your birthday cake. It's in the shape of Dad's bit of Antarctica. Just like your wildlife map.
SFX	Email beeps.
NARRATOR	A birthday email from Dad! Roo is upside down on the barge with a big R.T.A. on his bottom. Happy Birthday from the bottom of the world. R.T.A. means return to Australia That's what my Dad is going to do, soon.
SCHOOL KIDS' CHORUS & BRAD	(sing Happy Birthday and Narrator blows out the candles) (each of the choruses comes out and does their farewell dance) (ICEBERGS do a final roll to the music)

Part Scripts for Further Development

Groups of 4–5 students can use these ideas as the beginning of their own plays. They may need to 'borrow' people from other groups to perform once the script is worked out.

Using the same stimulus material, groups will develop very different versions. Much of the value of comparing the final versions lies in the discussion provoked on why and how people might react in those circumstances.

She Won't Be Coming Back

Setting

- A classroom on the day the school photograph is being taken.

Cast

- TEACHER
- LISA, the missing girl
- JANE, her best friend
- SAM, the boy whose desk is behind Lisa's desk
- CHILDREN'S CHORUS (any number)

Props

- Tables and chairs
- Photographs

Script Ideas

What happened to Lisa?

Did her parents move house?

Does she have to go to another school? Was Lisa hurt in a car accident?

Is she ill? Did she go to hospital?

If your friend left school suddenly, how would you feel? (Sad? Hurt that she didn't say goodbye?)

What would you say? (e.g. I miss Lisa. It's not fair.)

What would you do? (Ring her up? Write her a letter? Send a picture of what was happening in your class now? Send a class photo even if she isn't in it?)

What if Lisa never comes back?

Here are some feelings which students might express:

- I really miss Lisa at play time.
- We used to muck around together.
- Now I haven't got a best friend.
- It's not fair! She didn't tell me she was going away.
- My insides hurt when I think about her.
- Why did she leave me? I need her in the game.

How will your script finish?

Not In My Bed

An uncle, who is dying from cancer, is coming to stay with the family. Due to overcrowding, he'll sleep in Steve's bed. Steve is worried that the uncle will infect him.

Cast

- MOTHER
- STEVE
- TAMSIN, his sister
- UNCLE JIM
- CHORUS
- SFX This could be an audio play, with opening/closing music and other sound effects.

Script

MUM	Uncle Jim is coming to stay with us for the weekend.
STEVE	Why?
MUM	Because the train arrives on Friday night.
STEVE	Why does he have to stay with us?
TAMSIN	I'm going to a disco on Friday night. I won't be home.
STEVE	We've got a game on Saturday. I won't be here.
MUM	I'd like you to meet him first. Then you can go out.
TAMSIN	What's wrong with him? Why does he have to go to the hospital?
MUM	To have some special treatment.
STEVE	Why?
MUM	Because he's very sick.

STEVE	Is he going to die?
MUM	Maybe.
STEVE	He might die in my bed!
MUM	That's possible. We're all going to die some time.
STEVE	He'll have to sleep somewhere else.
TAMSIN	Can't he go to a motel or a caravan park?
MUM	Hospital costs a lot. He hasn't any spare money. Besides, he's my brother. We used to muck around at home together, like you and Tamsin.
STEVE	Did you fight?
MUM	Sometimes.
TAMSIN	How long since you've seen him?
MUM	Years. When you were babies.
STEVE	Why does he want to see you now?
MUM	I want to see him.
TAMSIN	I guess I'd want to see Steve again.
STEVE	If I never saw you again, that'd be okay.
SFX	(*knock at the door*)

Decide what happens next.

Who arrives?

What is said?

How can the Chorus be included?

How would you feel about someone who was dying coming to visit?

Would you treat them just the same as any other visitor?

Popstar

This story shares ways of coping with grief and the death of a grandparent. 'Popstar' is a story of love, death and grief, written for the family of a friend, Graham Brown. His grandkids called him Popstar.

Cast

- NARRATOR
- MUM
- DAD
- POP
- MIAOW THE CAT

Story

My family misses Pop.
I have a Mum and a Dad and a baby brother,
and a cat called Miaow,
and a dog with three legs called Woof.
And a Grandma, we Skype.
But we don't have Pop anymore.

I used to kick the ball with Pop.
He took me to the park.
And told me REALLY, REALLY bad jokes.
(Add your OWN bad joke here.)
And Pop built me a cubby house, but it fell down.
We made a vegetable garden, with just carrots.
Pop liked skinny, new carrots.
He ate them raw.
So did I.
He picked me up from school on Fridays.
And he always went to Grandparents & Special Friends' Day.
"I like the afternoon tea," said Pop. "Carrot cake."
"Did you like my drawings?" I asked.
"Of course. They were the best in the class."

A little while ago, he had to go to the doctor for some tests.
He stayed with us at our place for a week or so.
Miaow sat on his feet.
Woof chewed Pop's slippers.
Pop read me stories at night, if he wasn't too tired.

Then he went to hospital for a bit.
He lost his hair.
So he wore a cap.
Mum got Pop some Star Wars pyjamas.
Just like mine, only bigger.
I'm taller than Pop when he is lying down in bed.

"I'm bigger than you now."
Pop nodded.
We used to put marks on the cubby wall (before it fell down), to show how much I'd grown.
Sometimes I cheated and wore my BIG shoes.

"We have to drive Pop to hospital again" Mum said.
He was having chemo.
That zapped the bad cells in his body.
He looked a bit grey-white but he was still Pop.

Then the ambulance took Pop to hospital.
Beep Beep Beep.
Like a space ship, Pop's hospital bed had lines everywhere and a chart with his name on.
A bit scary.
"Don't come in again," said Pop to Mum. "Too hard to park."
So we rang him on his hospital bed phone for little chats.
"Hi Pop. Did you have afternoon tea?"
"Not today."
Miaow sat on his bed.

On Friday, Mum told me the REALLY bad news.

Pop had gone.

"Where has he gone?"

"Pop passed away."

"Where did he pass to?"

"He died."

"Can't he get up again, like the actors on TV?"

Mum shook her head. Her eyes looked weepy.

"The funeral will be on Monday."

"What's a funeral?"

"It's like a party for saying goodbye to someone you love.
Friends say nice things about the person."

"Why are you crying?"

"Because I won't see Pop any more."

"Where has he gone?"

"His body got very tired and wore out."

I get tired after footy but I have a sleep and I'm fine.

"Pop is going to sleep for a long time," says Mum.

I feel scared.

What if I don't wake up when I go to sleep?

That's a REALLY, REALLY bad worry.

So I stay awake for a long time.

Next night, Mum took me outside after dinner.

The sky was black but there were a few stars.

"Can you see that big star. Over there." Mum pointed.

"That's Pop's star. You can come out any night and talk to him. Tell him
what you have been doing."

"Will he fall out of the sky?"

Dad smiled. "No."

So Pop is still around.

We talk about the things he did.

His photo is framed on our family wall.

"Sometimes you laugh like Pop" says Mum.

Only when I tell Pop's REALLY bad jokes.

I remember them.

And I remember him.

When I crunch raw carrots.

Our carrots are still growing in the vegetable patch.

At the community centre, we put up a star on the Christmas tree for Pop.

And if I look up, at night, there's my Popstar.

Script Ideas

Could be this a monologue? What is a monologue and why are they used?

Students could adapt to a script and have a cast and chorus?

Read the story, develop a script and then perform it.

CONCLUSION

Grief is a natural response to loss. Grief has no set pattern. Everyone experiences grief differently. Some people may grieve for weeks and months, while others may describe their grief lasting for years.

Grief is something that takes time to work through. While everyone finds their own way to grieve it's important to have the support of friends and family, or someone else, and to talk about the loss when needed.

Many people do not know what to say or do when trying to comfort someone who is grieving. However, often it is the simple offer of love and support that is the most important.

- Ask how they're feeling. Each day can be different for someone who is grieving; take the time to listen and understand what they are going through.
- Talk about everyday life too. Their loss and grief does not have to be the focus of all your conversations.

- Ask them how you can help. A few home cooked meals, a little less homework or perhaps offering to do something enjoyable with them can all help someone through their grief.
- Encourage them to seek professional support if their grief does not seem to be easing over time.

We hope this provides you with a raft of practical ideas for your classroom and school.

CONTACTS

If you, a teaching colleague, a student or a school family needs further support in a difficult time you can contact:

Beyond Blue
www.beyondblue.org.au
1300 22 4636
The Beyond Blue Support Service provides 24/7 advice and support via telephone, webchat and email (email response provided within 24 hours).

Beyond Blue provides qualified mental health line counsellors, available to listen to you any time of day or night. Free, confidential telephone counselling (local call costs apply). Most calls last around 20 minutes.

LifeLine
www.lifeline.org.au
13 11 14
Access to crisis support, suicide prevention and mental health support services.

Australian Centre for Grief and Bereavement

www.grief.org.au

Information about grief and support for people who are grieving.

Head to Health

headtohealth.gov.au

Head to Health can help you find free and low-cost, trusted online and phone mental health resources.

GriefLine

www.griefline.org.au

1300 845 745

Grief helpline that provides telephone support services to individuals and families.